Japanese Business Dictionary

J APANESE BUSINESS DICTIONARY

ENGLISH to JAPANESE

Boye Lafayette De Mente

YENBOOKS

YENBOOKS are published and distributed
by the Charles E. Tuttle Company, Inc.
of Rutland, Vermont & Tokyo, Japan
with editorial offices at
2-6 Suido 1-chome, Bunkyo-ku, Tokyo 112

© 1991 by Boye De Mente

LCC Card No. 89–43535
ISBN 0-8048-1674-3

First edition, 1991
Second printing, 1991

Printed in Japan

Contents

Contents

How to Use This Dictionary

This book is designed to serve as a quick language reference for businesspeople dealing with the Japanese. It is particularly useful for those who must rely on their opposite party's English-language ability or the ability of their interpreters. There are times when one may wish to verify for oneself that certain crucial points are indeed being understood correctly. The *Japanese Business Dictionary* enables even those with little or no experience with the Japanese language to access specialized vocabulary, vocabulary that will allow them to get to the point immediately.

Of course, being able to pronounce the word or phrase correctly is also of great importance. To help achieve this goal, Japanese words and sentences in this book have been rendered in both standard Hepburn romanization and the author's time-tested phonetic system. One may use either system to attain correct pronunciation.

The Japanese language is based on combinations of only six key sounds, making it a fairly easy language to pronounce. These six sounds are the basis for an "alphabet" of some one hundred syllables that make up all the words in the Japanese language.

While there is only one way to pronounce Japanese properly, there are several ways to write it: using characters imported from China over one thousand years ago; using one of the two phonetic scripts called *kana* (kah-nah), devised by the Japanese to supplement and sometimes replace the Chinese ideograms; or using more familiar Roman letters, called *romaji* (roe-mah-jee) in Japanese.

The most widely used *romaji* system for transcribing Japanese was developed in the late 1800s by an American missionary, Dr. James Hepburn, soon after Japan's opening to the West. There are other Roman letter systems for writing Japanese, but Dr. Hepburn's was designed specifically for English speakers, and is therefore based on English phonetics.

All except one of the approximately one hundred syllables in the Japanese "alphabet" are based on the five (romanized) sounds: *a, i, u, e* and *o* — pronounced ah, ee, uu, ay, oh. The sixth base sound in the Japanese language is represented in English by the letter "n" and is pronounced like the "n" in the word "bond." As mentioned above, all Japanese words are made up of syllables consisting of combinations of these six basic sounds. The Japanese word for book, for example, is made up of two syllables, *ho* and *n* or *hon*, pronounced "hone" (rhyming with "bone"). The present tense of the word for read is *yomimasu*, is made up of four syllables—yo-mi-ma-su—although when said in ordinary speech, the last two syllables are typically run together, sounding like "mahss."

All Japanese syllables, with their English-language phonetic equivalents, are presented on the next page. To pronounce the syllables correctly, just read the phonetics (in parentheses) as if they were ordinary English sounds.

Basic Syllables and Sound Changes

a	i	u	e	o
(ah)	(ee)	(uu)	(ay)	(oh)
ka	ki	ku	ke	ko
(kah)	(kee)	(kuu)	(kay)	(koe)
sa	shi	su	se	so
(sah)	(she)	(sue)	(say)	(so)
ta	chi	tsu	te	to
(tah)	(chee)	(t'sue)	(tay)	(toe)
na	ni	nu	ne	no
(nah)	(nee)	(nuu)	(nay)	(no)
ha	hi	hu	he	ho
(hah)	(he)	(fuu)	(hay)	(hoe)
ma	mi	mu	me	mo
(mah)	(me)	(muu)	(may)	(moe)
ya		u		yo
(yah)		(uu)		(yoe)
ra	ri	ru	re	ro
(rah)	(ree)	(rue)	(ray)	(roe)
wa				wo
(wah)				(oh)

"n" (as the "n" in "bond")

ga	gi	gu	ge	go
(gah)	(ghee)	(guu)	(gay)	(go)
za	ji	zu	ze	zo
(zah)	(jee)	(zuu)	(zay)	(zoe)
da	ji	zu	de	do
(dah)	(jee)	(zuu)	(day)	(doe)
ba	bi	bu	be	bo
(bah)	(bee)	(buu)	(bay)	(boe)
pa	pi	pu	pe	po
(pah)	(pee)	(puu)	(pay)	(poe)

The following thirty-three syllables are combinations of some of those appearing in the two sets above. The first syllable, for example, is a combination of *ki* and *ya*, or *kiya*, phonetically shortened to *kya*. The last syllable, *pyo*, is a combination of *pi* and *yo*, similarly shortened.

kya	kyu	kyo
(k'yah)	(cue)	(k'yoe)
sha	shu	sho
(shah)	(shuu)	(show)
cha	chu	cho
(chah)	(chuu)	(choe)
nya	nyu	nyo
(n'yah)	(n'yuu)	(n'yoe)
hya	hyu	hyo
(h'yah)	(h'yuu)	(h'yoe)
mya	myu	myo
(m'yah)	(m'yuu)	(m'yoe)
rya	ryu	ryo
(r'yah)	(r'yuu)	(rio)
gya	gyu	gyo
(g'yah)	(g'yuu)	(g'yoe)
ja	ju	jo
(jah)	(juu)	(joe)
bya	byu	byo
(b'yah)	(b'yuu)	(b'yoe)
pya	pyu	pyo
(p'yah)	(p'yuu)	(p'yoe)

While you are becoming familiar with the pronunciation of the various syllables in the Japanese "alphabet" by reading the phonetics aloud, be sure also to familiarize yourself with the Hepburn spelling of each syllable so you can recognize words written in *romaji*.

As you probably noticed, a combination of two or more Japanese syllables often forms the sound of some common English word. For example, the combination of *sa* and *i (sai)* is pronounced exactly like the word "sigh." *Hai,* meaning "yes," is pronounced "high." Such words, instead of the phonetic spellings, have frequently been used in this dictionary to facilitate pronunciation.

After you read a word or phrase slowly a few times out loud (always out loud!), practice saying it at ordinary speaking speed to get away from the "textbook sound." In any event, don't be bashful about using the Japanese you learn. Simply by using individual words, you can communicate to a useful and often surprising extent.

Special Language Pointers

There are no definite or indefinite articles in Japanese. There is also usually no differentiation made between the singular and plural form of nouns. *Hako* (hah-koe) can be one box or two or more boxes, depending on the context. The number of a noun is usually made clear by context, but there are also special suffixes to express plurals, particularly common with personal pronouns. For example, *tachi* (tah-chee) added to the pronouns *I, he,* and *she* gives *we* and *they:*

I – *watakushi* (wah-tock-she)
We – *watakushi-tachi* (wah-tock-she-tah-chee)
You – *anata* (ah-nah-tah)
You (plural) – *anata-tachi* (ah-nah-tah-tah-chee); or the polite form *anata-gata* (ah-nah-tah-gah-tah)
He – *kare* (kah-ray); *ano hito* (ah-no-shtoe); or the polite form *ano kata* (ah-no-kah-tah)
She – *kanojo* (kah-no-joe); or *ano hito* (ah-no-shtoe)
They – *ano hito-tachi* (ah-no-shtoe); *kare-tachi* (kah-ray-tah-chee) or *kanojo-tachi* (kah-no-joe-tah-chee); the polite form *anokata-gata* (ah-no-kah-tah-gah-tah)

The interrogative form is expressed in Japanese by *ka* (kah) at the end of a verb or sentence.

The order of a Japanese sentence is subject/object/verb, as opposed to the English order of subject/verb/object. Because the verb comes last in a Japanese sentence one must wait until the sentence is completed before knowing whether it is affirmative or negative.

An important point to keep in mind is not to be overly concerned with differences in Japanese and English grammar. Especially if you are a beginner, the best idea is to forget about grammar and simply learn Japanese sentences as they are spoken. With repetition, Japanese sentence structure will also sound perfectly natural.

Another point to keep in mind is that the subject is often left out in Japanese sentences, the message expressed with only the verb. For example: the present tense of the verb "to go" *ikimasu* (ee-kee-mahss) means "go" or "going, am going," or "will go." By adding *ka* to it *(ikimasu ka?)*, it becomes "are you going?" Japanese often use various verb forms as whole sentences. With just the various tenses of *ikimasu*, for example, you can say the following:

Ikimasu. (ee-kee-mahss) – I am going.
Ikimasen. (ee-kee-mah-sen) – I'm not going. / He/she is
    not going. / They are not going.
Ikimasen deshita. (ee-kee-mah-sen desh-tah) –
    I/he/she/they did not go.
Ikimashō. (ee-kee-mah-show) – Let's go.
Ikimashita. (ee-kee-mah-shtah) – I/he/she/they went.

Three of the primary building blocks of ideas or sentences in Japanese are *desu* (dess), the verb "to be," *aru* (ah-rue), which means "have" as well as expressing the idea of "to be"; and *iru* (ee-rue), which expresses both existence and "being" as well as ongoing action when it follows a verb.

Desu (dess) expresses the indicative present "is" and, unlike the other "to be/there are" verbs, is never used by itself. The past tense of *desu* is *deshita* (desh-tah). The polite negative is *de wa arimasen* (day wah ah-ree-mah-sen). In everyday speech this is often abbreviated to *de wa nai* (day wah nigh), and in familiar speech to *ja nai* (jah nigh).

That is expensive.
  Sore wa takai desu.
  (so-ray wah tah-kye dess)
That is not expensive.
  Sore wa takaku arimasen.
  (so-ray wah tah-kah-kuu ah-ree-mah-sen)
  Sore wa takaku wa nai.
  (so-ray wah tah-kah-kuu wah nigh)
  Sore wa takaku nai.
  (so-ray wah tah-kah-kuu nigh)

Both *aru* (ah-rue) and *iru* (ee-rue) can be used by themselves as well as being used in combination with other verbs. *Aru* is used when you want to make a "have" or "there is" statement or ask a "have you" or "is there" question. When used just by itself *aru* conveys the idea of "I have" or "there is." When *iru* is used by itself it generally refers to people or other living things being present at that location or somewhere else.

Another word that will get you a long way in Japanese is *kudasai* (kuu-dah-sigh), which has the meaning of "please do" (something) or "please give" (something) and is used as an ending for verbs and following nouns.

Mizu wo kudasai. (me-zuu oh kuu-dah-sigh) – Water, please. (Please give me water.)
Pan wo kudasai. (pahn oh kuu-dah-sigh) – Bread, please.
Tabete kudasai. (tah-bay-tay kuu-dah-sigh) – Please eat.

He was killed in a car accident.
Ano hito wa jidōsha jiko de shinimashita.
(ah-no shtoe wah jee-doe-shah jee-koe day she-nee-mahsh-tah)

I met her by accident.
Kanojo ni gūzen aimashita.
(kah-no-joe nee guu-zen eye-mahsh-tah)

accidental damage – *gūhatsu teki songai* (guu-hot-sue tay-kee soan-guy)

accident insurance – *shōgai hoken* (show-guy hoe-ken)

What kind of accident insurance do you have?
Donna shōgai hoken ga arimasu ka?
(doan-nah show-guy hoe-ken gah ah-ree-mahss kah)

accompany (go with) – *issho ni iku* (ee-show nee ee-kuu); (see off) – *miokuri suru* (me-oh-kuu-ree sue-rue)

I will go with you.
Issho ni ikimasu.
(ee-show-nee ee-kee-mahss)

I will accompany you to the airport.
Kūkō made o-miokuri shimasu.
(kuu-koe mah-day oh-me-oh-kuu-ree she-mahss)

Please come with me.
Watakushi to issho ni kite kudasai.
(wah-tock-she toe ee-show-nee kee-tay kuu-dah-sigh)

account (statement of money) – *kanjō* (kahn-joe); calculation – *keisan* (kay-sahn)

Please bring the bill.
O-kanjō wo motte kite kudasai.
(oh-kahn-joe oh moat-tay kee-tay kuu-dah-sigh)

I'll pay it now.
Ima haraimasu.
(ee-mah hah-rye-mahss)

Please add up my bill.

Watakushi no o-kanjō wo keisan shite kudasai.
(wah-tock-she no oh-kahn-joe oh kay-sahn shtay kuu-dah-sigh)

Add it to my bill.

O-kanjō ni tsukete oite kudasai.
(oh-kahn-joe nee skay-tay oh-ee-tay kuu-dah-sigh)

accountability (management) – *keiei sekinin* (kay-ay say-kee-neen)

accountant – *kaikei gakari* (kye-kay gah-kah-ree)

accountant, chief – *kaikei shunin* (kye-kay shuu-neen)

account balance – *torihiki kanjō zandaka* (toe-ree-he-kee kahn-joe zahn-dah-kah)

account, current – *tōza kanjō* (toe-zah kahn-joe)

account executive (advertising) – *akaunto eguzekutibu* (ah-count-oh egg-zay-kuu-tee-buu)

account executive (securities) – *shōken gaisha eigyō buin* (show-ken guy-shah ay-g'yoe buu-een)

accounting department – *kaikei bu* (kye-kay buu)

accounting method – *kaikei hōshiki* (kye-kay hoe-she-kee)

accounting period – *kaikei kikan* (kye-kay kee-kahn)

When does your (company) accounting period start?

Kaisha no kaikei kikan wa itsu hajimarimasu ka?
(kye-shah no kye-kay kee-kahn wah eat-sue hah-jee-mah-ree-mahss kah)

account number – *kōza bangō* (koe-zah bahn-go)

Please write your account number here.

Koko ni kōza bangō wo kaite kudasai.
(koe-koe nee koe-zah bahn-go oh kye-tay kuu-dah-sigh)

What is your account number?

Kōza bangō wa nan desu ka?
(koe-zah bahn-go wah nahn dess ka)

accounts payable – *shiharai kanjō* (she-hah-rye kahn-joe)

accounts receivable – *uketori kanjō* (uu-kay-toe-ree kahn-joe)

accounts secured – *tanpo tsuki kanjō* (tahn-poe ski kahn-joe)

accrual – *keika rishi* (kay-kah ree-she)

accrual method – *hassei shugi hō* (hah-say shuu-ghee hoe)

accumulated depreciation – *genka shō kyaku ruikei gaku* (gen-kah show kyah-kuu ruee-ee-kay-gah-kuu)

acknowledge – *mitomeru* (me-toe-may-rue)

acknowledge receipt of – *uketori o mitomeru* (uu-kay-toe-ree oh me-toe-may-rue)

acquired rights – *kitoku ken* (kee-toe-kuu ken)

acquisition – *shutoku* (shuu-toe-kuu)

acquisition cost – *shutoku genka* (shuu-toe-kuu gen-kah)

acronym – *kashira moji-go* (kah-she-rah moe-jee-go)

across-the-board settlement – *zenmen teki ketchaku* (zen-men tay-kee kay-chah-kuu)

action plan – *jikkō keikaku* (jeek-koe kay-kah-kuu)

active account – *katsudō kanjō* (kah-t'sue-doe kahn-joe)

active debt – *katsudō fusai* (kah-t'sue-doe fuu-sigh)

active trust – *sekkyoku shintaku* (sake-k'yoe-kuu sheen-tah-kuu)

activity chart – *katsudō chōsa hyō* (kah-t'sue-doe choe-sah h'yoe)

act of God – *fuka kōryoku* (fuu-kah koe-rio-kuu)

actual cash value – *genkin kanka kachi* (gen-keen kahn-kah kah-chee)

actual cost – *jissai genka* (jeece-sigh gen-kah)

actual income – *jisshūnyū* (jeesh-shune-yuu)

added cost – *kosuto zō* (koe-stow zoe)

add-on sales – *kappu hanbai* (kahp-puu hahn-buy)

addressee – *na-ate-nin* (nah-ah-tay-neen)
    Are you the addressee?
        Anata na-ate-nin desu ka?
        (ah-nah-tah wah nah-ah-tay-neen dess kah)

adjusted CIF price – *chōsei zumi hoken ryō unchin komi nedan* (choe-say zuu-me hoe-ken rio uun-cheen koe-me nay-dahn)

adjusted earned income – *chōsei zumi kinrō shotoku* (choe-say zuu-me keen-roe show-toe-kuu)

administrative – *kanri no* (kahn-ree no)

administrative expense – *ippan kanri hi* (eep-pahn kahn-ree he)

administrative guidance – *gyōsei shidō* (g'yoe-say she-doe)*
    *(This term refers to guidelines and suggestions made by various government agencies and ministries to Japan's business world)

administrator – *keiei sha* (kay-ay shah)

advanced country – *senshin koku* (sen-sheen koe-kuu)

advanced technology – *senshin gijutsu* (sen-sheen ghee-jute-sue); *sentan gijutsu* (sen-tahn ghee-jute-sue)

advance freight payment – *mae barai unchin* (my bah-rye uun-cheen)

advance notice – *yokoku* (yoe-koe-kuu)
    Please give two weeks advance notice.
        Nishūkan mae ni yokoku wo shite kudasai.
        (nee-shuu-kahn my nee yoe-koe-kuu oh shtay kuu-dah-sigh)

advance payment – *maekin barai* (my-keen bah-rye); *saki barai* (sah-kee bah-rye)
    You must pay in advance.

Maekin de harawanakereba narimasen.
(my-keen day hah-rah-wah-nah-kay-ray-bah nah-ree-mah-sen)
I will pay in advance.
Maekin de haraimasu.
(my-keen day hah-rye-mahss)

advantage – *rieki* (ree-ay-kee); to take advantage of, avail oneself of – *riyō suru* (ree-yoe sue-rue)
This contract is definitely to your advantage.
Kono keiyaku wa tashika ni anata no go-rieki ni narimasu.
(koe-no kay-yah-kuu wah tah-she-kah nee ah-nah-tah no go-ree-ay-kee nee nah-ree-mahss)
Let's take advantage of this occasion.
Kono kikai wo riyō shimashō.
(koe-no kee-kye oh ree-yoe she-mah-show)

adverse import balance – *yunyū chōka* (yuun-yuu choe-kah)

advertise – *kōkoku (wo) suru* (koe-koe-kuu oh sue-rue);
place an ad – *kōkoku wo dasu* (koe-koe-kuu oh dah-sue)
Please put this ad in the Sunday paper.
Kono kōkoku wo nichiyōbi no shinbun ni dashite kudasai.
(koe-no koe-koe-kuu oh nee-chee-yoe-bee no sheem-boon nee dah-shtay kuu-dah-sigh)
How much will the advertisement cost?
Kōkoku wa ikura shimasu ka?
(koe-koe-kuu wah ee-kuu-rah she-mahss kah)

advertisement (request) for bid – *nyūsatsu kōkoku* (nyuu-sah-t'sue koe-koe-kuu)

advertising – *kōkoku* (koe-koe-kuu)

advertising agency – *kōkoku dairiten* (koe-koe-kuu dye-ree-ten)

advertising budget – *kōkoku hi yosan* (koe-koe-kuu he yoe-sahn)

advertising campaign – *kōkoku sen* (koe-koe-kuu sen)

advertising drive – *senden urikomi* (sen-den uu-ree-koe-me)

advertising expenses – *kōkoku hi* (koe-koe-kuu he)

advertising manager – *kōkoku buchō* (koe-koe-kuu buu-choe)

advertising media – *kōkoku baitai* (koe-koe-kuu by-tie); *kōkoku mejia* (koe-koe-kuu may-jee-ah)

advertising rate – *kōkoku ryō* (koe-koe-kuu rio)
   What is the advertising rate for one page?
      Ichi peji no kōkoku ryō wa ikura desu ka?
      (ee-chee pay-jee no koe-koe-kuu rio wah ee-kuu-rah dess kah)

advertising research – *kōkoku chōsa* (koe-koe-kuu choe-sah)

advisor (consultant) – *sōdan-aite* (so-dahn-eye-tay); counselor – *sōdan-yaku* (so-dahn-yah-kuu); legal advisor – *hōritsu komon* (hoe-ree-t'sue koe-moan)
   I would like to introduce you to our company adviser.
      Uchi no kaisha no sōdan-yaku wo go-shōkai shimasu.
      (uu-chee no kye-shah no so-dahn-yah-kuu oh go-show-kye she-mahss)

advisory committee – *shingi kai* (sheen-ghee kye)
   The advisory committee is meeting tomorrow at ten.
      Shingi kai wa ashita jū ji kara desu.
      (sheen-ghee kye wah ah-shtah juu jee kah-rah dess)

advisory council – *shimon kaigi* (she-moan kye-ghee)

affidavit – *sensei kyōjutsu sho* (sen-say k'yoe-jute-sue show)

affiliate – *keiretsu gaisha* (kay-rate-sue guy-shah)

affiliated company – *keiretsu gaisha* (kay-rate-sue guy-shah)
Do you have any affiliated companies in the U.S.?
Amerika ni keiretsu gaisha ga arimasu ka?
(ah-may-ree-kah nee kay-rate-sue guy-shah gah ah-ree-mahss kah)

affiliation – *teikei* (tay-kay)

affirm; confirm – *kakuritsu suru* (kah-kuu-ree-t'sue sue-rue); *kakunin suru* (kah-kuu-neen sue-rue)
I would like to confirm my reservations.
Yoyaku wo kakunin shitai desu.
(yoe-yah-kuu oh kah-kuu-neen she-tie dess)

after-hours trading – *jikan gai torihiki* (jee-kahn guy toe-ree-he-kee)

after-sale service – *afutā sābisu* (ah-fuu-tah sah-be-sue)
After-sale service is very important to customers.
O-kyakusan ni afutā sābisu wa taisetsu na koto desu.
(oh-kyack-sahn nee ahf-tah sah-bee-sue wah tie-say-t'sue nah koe-toe dess)

after-tax income – *zeibiki go shotoku* (zay-bee-kee go show-toe-kuu)

after-tax profit – *zeibiki rieki* (zay-bee-kee ree-ay-kee)

after-tax real rate of return – *zeibiki rieki ritsu* (zay-bee-kee ree-ay-kee ree-t'sue)

against all risks (insurance) – *zen kiken tanpo de* (zen kee-ken tahn-poe day)

agency; agent (company) – *dairi ten* (dye-ree ten)

agency fee – *dairi ten tesūryō* (dye-ree-ten tay-sue-rio)

agenda – *kyōgi jikō* (k'yoe-ghee jee-koe)

agent (company) – *dairiten* (dye-ree-ten)

agent (person) – *dairinin* (dye-ree-neen)

agree – *sansei suru* (sahn-say sue-rue); *dōkan suru* (doe-kahn sue-rue)

I cannot agree to that.
  Sore niwa sansei dekimasen.
  (so-ray nee-wah sahn-say day-kee-mah-sen)
agreement; treaty – *kyōtei* (k'yoe-tay); commercial
  agreement – *shōgyō kyōtei* (show-g'yoe k'yoe-tay)
  I have reached an agreement with Shinwa Boeki.
  Shinwa Bōeki to kyōtei ga seiritsu shimashita.
  (sheen-wah boe-ay-kee toe k'yoe-tay gah say-ree-
  t'sue she-mahsh-tah)
agricultural land – *nōchi* (no-chee)
  Agricultural land in Japan is rapidly decreasing.
  Nihon wa nōchi wo hayaku herashite imasu.
  (nee-hone wah no-chee oh hah-yah-kuu hay-rah-
  shtay ee-mahss)
agricultural products – *nōsanbutsu* (no-sahn-boot-
  sue)
agriculture – *nōgyō* (no-g'yoe)
  Agriculture is still very important to Japan.
  Nihon de wa nōgyō wa mada jūyō desu.
  (nee-hone day wah no-g'yoe wah mah-dah juu-yoe
  dess)
agriculture and forestry – *nōrin* (no-reen)
aid; assist – *enjo* (en-joe); to aid – *enjo suru* (en-joe
  sue-rue); *sewa* (say-wah)
  I really appreciate your assistance.
  Anata no enjo wo hontō ni kansha shimasu.
  (ah-nah-tah no en-joe oh hone-toe nee kahn-shah
  she-mahss)
air conditioner (for auto) – *kā eakon* (kah ay-ah-cone)
air express – *kōkū sokutatsu bin* (koe-kuu so-kuu-tah-
  t'sue bean)
air freight – *kōkū kamotsu yusō* (koe-kuu kah-moe-
  t'sue yuu-so)
airmail – *ea mēru* (ay-ah may-rue); *kōkū bin* (koe-kuu
  bean)

Please send it airmail.

Ea mēru de okutte kudasai.

(ay-ah may-rue day oh-coot-tay kuu-dah-sigh)

airport – *kūkō* (kuu-koe)

air shipment – *kūyu* (kuu-yuu)

a la carte – *ippin ryōri* (eep-peen rio-ree); full course –
furu kōsu (fuu-rue koe-sue)

I'll take the full course.

Furu kōsu ni shimasu.

(fuu-rue koe-sue nee she-mahss)

all; entire – *zenbu* (zem-buu)

Is this all?

Kore de zembu desu ka?

(koe-ray day zem-buu dess kah)

all in cost – *sō genka* (so gen-kah)

allocation of responsibilities – *sekinin buntan* (say-
kee-neen boon-tahn)

allotment; quota – *wariate* (wah-ree-ah-tay)

I have already used up my allotment.

Wariate wo mō tsukatte shimaimashita.

(wah-ree-ah-tay oh moe scot-tay she-my-mahsh-
tah)

allowance (finance) – *hikiate kin* (he-kee-ah-tay keen)

allowance/discount (sales) – *waribiki* (wah-ree-bee-
kee)

allowances (additional pay) – *teate* (tay-ah-tay); allowance for children – *fuyō teate* (fuu-yoe tay-ah-tay);
cost-of-living allowance – *seikatsu teate* (say-kah-
t'sue tay-ah-tay); transportation allowance – *kōtsū hi*
(koe-t'sue-he); retirement allowance – *taishoku teate*
(tie-show-kuu tay-ah-tay); end-of-year allowance –
nenmatsu teate (kee-mah-t'sue tay-ah-tay); supervi-
sory position allowance – *kanri shoku teate* (kahn-ree
show-kuu tay-ah-tay)

alteration/change – *henkō* (hen-koe)

alternating current – *kōryū* (koe-r'yuu)

amend; alter – *henkō suru* (hen-koe sue-rue)
  I would like to amend this agreement.
  Kono kyōtei wo henkō shitai desu.
  (koe-no k'yoe-tay oh hen-koe she-tie dess)

amendment; revision – *shūsei* (shuu-say)
  I would like to have an amendment added to the
  agreement.
  Kyōtei ni shūsei wo tsukekuwaete itadakitai desu.
  (k'yoe-tay nee shuu-say oh t'sue-kay-kuu-why-tay
  ee-tah-dah-kee-tie dess)

American Club – *Amerikan Kurabu* (ah-may-ree-
kahn kuu-rah-buu)

American Embassy – *Amerika Taishikan* (ah-may-
ree-kah tie-she-kahn)

amortization – *nenpu shōkan* (nen-puu show-kahn)

amount – *sōgaku* (so-gah-kuu)

amount due – *manki shiharai daka* (mahn-kee she-
hah-rye dah-kah)

amplifier – *zōfuku ki* (zoe-fuu-kuu kee); *anpu* (ahn-
puu)

analysis – *bunseki* (boon-say-kee)
  I would like to hear your analysis at our next conference.
  *Tsugi no kaigi de anata no bunseki wo kikitai desu
  ga.*
  (t'sue no kye-ghee day ah-nah-tah no boon-say-kee
  oh kee-kee-tie dess gah)

analysis (of a competitor) – *kyōgō sha bunseki* (k'yoe-
go shah boon-say-kee)

analysis, cost – *genka bunseki* (gen-kah boon-say-kee)

analysis, financial – *zaimu bunseki* (zye-muu boon-
say-kee)

analysis, product – *seihin bunseki* (say-heen boon-
say-kee)

analysis, sales – *hanbai bunseki* (hahn-by boon-say-kee)

analysis, system – *shisutemu bunseki* (she-stay-muu boon-say-kee)

analyst – *bunseki-sha* (boon-say-kee-shah)

announcement (communique) – *happyō* (hop-p'yoe); statement – *seimei* (say-may); notice – *tsūkoku* (t'sue-koe-kuu)

I will make a statement tomorrow.
Ashita seimei wo happyō shimasu.
(ah-shtah say-may oh hop-p'yoe she-mahss)

annual (per year) – *nenkan* (nen-kahn)

The association publishes the results annually.
Kyōkai wa nenkan no kekka wo shuppan shimasu.
(k'yoe-kye wah nen-kahn no kay-kah oh shuu-pahn she-mahss)

annual accounts – *nenji kessan hōkoku* (nen-jee kay-sahn hoe-koe-kuu)

annual audit – *nenji kaikei kensa* (nen-jee kye-kay ken-sah)

annual expenditures – *nenji saishutsu* (nen-jee sigh-shoot-sue)

annual income – *nen shū* (nen shuu)

annual report – *nenji eigyō hōkokusho* (nen-jee ay-g'yoe hoe-koe-kuu-show)

annuity – *nenkin* (nen-keen)

answer – *henji* (hen-jee)

Please give me an answer at your earliest convenience.
Dōzo, go-tsugō ga tsukishidai go-henji wo kudasai.
(doe-zoe go-t'sue-go gah t'sue-kee-she-dye go-henjee oh kuu-dah-sigh)

antenna – *antena* (ahn-tay-nah)

anti-depression cartel – *fukyō karuteru* (fuu-k'yoe kah-rue-tay-rue)

antitrust laws – *dokusen kinshi hō* (doke-sen keen-she hoe)

apartment – *apāto* (ah-pah-toe)

apartment complex (building for ordinary workers) – *danchi* (dahn-chee)

apartment in deluxe condo style – *manshon* (mahn-shone)

apologize – *ayamaru* (ah-yah-mah-rue); *wabiru* (wah-bee-rue); *yurusu* (yuu-rue-sue)

I must apologize to you.
   Watashi wa anata ni ayamaranakereba narimasen.
   (wah-tock-she wah ah-nah-tah nee ah-yah-mah-rah-nah-kay-ray-bah nah-ree-mah-sen)

I owe you an apology.
   Anata ni o-wabi wo shinakereba narimasen.
   (ah-nah-tah nee oh-wah-bee oh she-nah-kay-ray-bah nah-ree-mah-sen)

Please accept my apologies.
   Dōzo, o-yurushi kudasai.
   (doe-zoe oh-yuu-rue-she kuu-dah-sigh)

apology – *mōshiwake* (moe-she-wah-kay)

I apologize (I have no excuse).
   Mōshiwake arimasen.
   (moe-she-wah-kay ah-ree-mah-sen)

applicant – *shigansha* (she-gahn-shah)

Have all of the applicants arrived?
   Shigansha wa zenbu tsukimashita ka?
   (she-gahn-shah wa zem-buu t'sue-kee-mahsh-tah kah)

application form – *mōshikomi sho* (moe-she-koe-me show); *shinsei sho* (sheen-say show)

apply for; application – *mōshikomu* (moe-she-koe-muu)

Please apply at that office.
   Ano jimusho e mōshikonde kudasai.

(ah-no jeem-show ay moe-she-kone-day kuu-dah-
  sigh)

appointment (engagement) – *yakusoku* (yah-kuu-so-
kuu)

appraisal – *hyōka* (h'yoe-kah)

appreciate – *kansha suru* (kahn-shah sue-rue)
  I really appreciate having your support in this situa-
  tion.
    Anata no go-shien wo hontō ni kansha shimasu.
    (ah-nah-tah no go-she-en oh hone-toe nee kahn-
    shah she-mahss)

appreciation (rise in value) – *kakaku tōki* (kah-kah-
kuu toe-kee)

apprentice – *minarai* (me-nah-rye)

approval – *ninka* (neen-kah); *kyoka* (k'yoe-kah); to approve – *sansei suru* (sahn-say sue-rue)
  I approve.
    Sansei shimasu.
    (sahn-say she-mahss)

approved delivery facility – *ninka zumi*
  hikiwatashi shisetsu (neen-kah zuu-me he-kee-wah-
  tah-she she-say-t'sue)

arbitration (mediation) – *chōtei* (choe-tay); *chūsai*
  suru (chew-sigh sue-rue)
  Please mediate this dispute.
    Kono funsō wo chūsai shite kudasai.
    (koe-no fuun-so oh chew-sigh shtay kuu-dah-sigh)

arbitration agreement – *chūsai kyōtei* (chew-sigh
k'yoe-tay)

arbitrator – *chūsai-nin* (chew-sigh-neen)

area (region, zone) – *chiiki* (chee-ee-kee)
  Are there any factories in that region?
    Sono chiiki ni kōjō ga arimasu ka?
    (so-no chee-ee-kee nee koe-joh gah ah-ree-mahss
    kah)

area manager – *chiiki tantō shihai-nin* (chee-ee-kee tahn-toe she-high-neen)

argument – *giron* (ghee-roan); *ii-arasou* (ee-ah-rah-so)

An argument started.

Giron ga demashita.

(ghee-roan gah day-mahsh-tah)

I want to avoid arguing about the price.

Dekireba kakaku no koto de ii-arasou no wa saketai desu.

(day-kee-ray-bah kah-kah-kuu no koe-toe day ee-ah-rah-so no wah sah-kay-tie dess)

arm's length – *aitai torihiki* (eye-tie toe-ree-he-kee)

arrange; arrangement – *tehai suru* (tay-high sue-rue)

I'll arrange it.

Tehai wa shimasu.

(tay-high wah she-mahss)

Can you arrange a car?

Kuruma wo tehai dekimasu ka?

(kuu-rue-mah oh tay-high day-kee-mahss kah)

Arrangements have been completed.

Tehai wa kanryō shiteimasu.

(tah-high wah kahn-rio shtay-mahss)

Have you finished the arrangements?

Tehai wa owarimashita ka?

(tay-high wah oh-wah-ree-mahsh-tah kah)

arrears – *tainō kin* (tie-no keen)

arrival gate – *tōchaku guchi* (toe-chah-kuu guu-chee)

What is the number of his arrival gate?

Tōchaku guchi wa nanban desu ka?

(kah-ray no toe-chah-kuu guu-chee wah nahn-bahn dess kah)

arrive safely (goods) – *anchaku* (ahn-chah-kuu)

The goods arrived safely.

Shinamono wa anchaku shimashita.

(she-nah-moe-no wah ahn-chah-kuu she-mahsh-
tah)

arriving passengers – *tōchaku kyaku* (toe-chah-kuu
k'yah-kuu)

Where will the arriving passengers exit from?
  Tōchaku kyaku wa doko kara detekimasu ka?
  (toe-chah-kuu k'yah-kuu wah doe-koe kah-rah day-
  tay-kee-mahss kah)

articles of association (for formation of a company) –
teikan (tay-kahn)

asking price – *iine* (ee-nay)

aspect – *men* (men)

There are several aspects to the problem.
  Mondai ni wa iro iro na men ga arimasu.
  (moan-dye nee wah ee-roe ee-roe nah men gah ah-
  ree-mahss)

assay – *bunseki* (boon-say-kee)

assemble (a product) – *kumitateru* (kuu-me-tah-tay-
rue)

assembly factory – *kumitate kōjō* (kuu-me-tah-tay
koe-joe)

assembly line – *nagare sagyō retsu* (nah-gah-ray sah-
g'yoe rate-sue)

assembly operation – *kumitate sagyō* (kuu-me-tah-
tay sah-g'yoe)

Please assemble this radio.
  Kono rajio wo kumitatete kudasai.
  (koe-noe rah-jee-oh oh kuu-me-tah-tay-tay kuu-dah-
  sigh)

asset – *shisan* (she-sahn)

assets, fixed – *kotei shisan* (koe-tay she-sahn)

assets, intangible – *mukei shisan* (muu-kay she-sahn)

assets, liquid – *ryūdō shisan* (ree-yuu-doe she-sahn)

assets, net – *jun shisan* (june she-sahn)

assets, tangible – *yūkei shisan* (yuu-kay she-sahn)

assistance; aid – *enjo* (en-joe)
Can you assist that woman?
> *Sono onna-no-hito wo enjo dekimasu ka?*
> (so-no own-nah-no-shtoe oh en-joe day-kee-mahss kah)

assistant – *joshu* (joe-shuu)

assistant general manager – *fuku sō shihai-nin* (fuu-kuu so she-high-neen)

assistant manager – *fuku shihai-nin* (fuu-kuu she-high-neen)

assistant section manager – *kakarichō* (kah-kah-ree-choe)

associate company – *kanren gaisha* (kahn-ren guy-shah)

association – *kyōkai* (k'yoe-kye)
What is the name of the association?
> *Kyōkai no namae wa nan desu ka?*
> (k'yoe-kye no nah-my wah nahn dess kah)

Association of Japanese Employers (one of the most important business organizations in Japan) – *Nikkeiren* (nee-kay-ren)

assortment of goods – *toriawase* (toe-ree-ah-wah-say)

as usual – *aikawarazu* (eye-kah-wah-rah-zuu)
I'm fine, as usual.
> *Aikawarazu genki desu.*
> (eye-kah-wah-rah-zuu gen-kee dess)

atomic age – *genshi-ryoku jidai* (gen-she-rio-kuu jee-dye)

atomic energy – *genshi ryoku* (gen-she rio-kuu)

at par – *heika de* (hay-kah day)

at sight – *ichiran barai de* (ee-chee-rahn bah-rye day)

attachment – *fuzoku-hin* (fuu-zoe-kuu-heen)
Do you know where the computer attachments are?
> *Konpyūta no fuzoku-hin wa doko ni iru ka shitteimasu ka?*

(koe-no comb-pew-tah no fuu-zoe-kuu-heen wah
doe-koe nee ee-rue kah shtay-ee-mahss kah)

attend; attendance – *shusseki* (shuus-say-kee)
How many people will attend?
Nannin ga shusseki shimasu ka?
(nahn-neen gah shuus-say-kee she-mahss kah)

attitude – *taido* (tie-doe)
I do not like his attitude.
Ano hito no taido wa suki ja nai desu.
(ah-no shtoe no tie-doe wah ski jah nigh dess)

attorney – *bengoshi* (ben-go-she)

attorney, power of – *ininken* (ee-neen-ken)

attrition – *jin-in sakugen* (jeen-een sah-kuu-gen)

auction – *kyōbai* (k'yoe-by); *seriuri* (say-ree-uu-ree)

audio component system – *ōdio konpo* (oh-dee-oh
cone-poe)

audio response equipment – *onsei ōtō sōchi* (own-
say oh-toe so-chee)

audit (verb) – *kaikei kansa suru* (kye-kay kahn-sah
sue-rue)

auditing balance sheet – *kansa taishaku taishō hyō*
(kahn-sah tie-shah-kuu tie-show h'yoe)

auditor – *kaikei kansa nin* (kye-kay kahn-sah neen)

Australian Embassy – *Ōsutoraria Taishikan* (oh-sue-
toe-rah-ree-ah tie-she-kahn)

authority; power – *kenryoku* (ken-rio-kuu)
Who is the man with the power?
Kenryoku no aru hito wa dare desu ka?
(ken-rio-kuu no ah-rue shtoe wah dah-ray dess kah)

authorize – *kengen wo ataeru* (ken-gen oh ah-tie-rue)

authorized agent – *shitei dairiten* (she-tay dye-ree-
ten)

authorized dealer – *kōnin toriatsukai gyōsha* (koe-
neen toe-ree-ah-t'sue-kye g'yoe-shah)

authorized shares – *nintei kabu* (neen-tay kah-buu)

authorized signature – *seishiki no shomei* (say-she-kee no show-may)

auto-checker – *ōto-chekkā* (oh-toe check-kah)

automate – *ōtomēshon suru* (oh-toe-may-shone sue-rue)

Can you automate this step?

Kono dankai wo ōtomēshon dekimasu ka?
(koe-no dahn-kye oh oh-toe-may-shone day-kee-mahss kah)

automatic – *jidō* (jee-doe); *jidōteki* (jee-doe-tay-kee)

In Japan taxi doors are automatic.

Nihon dewa takushi no doa wa jidō desu.
(nee-hone day-wah tah-kuu-she no doe-ah wah jee-doe dess)

automatic gearshift – *ōto kurachi* (oh-toe kuu-rah-chee)

automatic transmission – *jidō hensoku-ki* (jee-doe-shah hen-so-kuu-kee)

automation – *ōtomēshon* (oh-toe-may-shone)

automobile – *jidōsha* (jee-doe-shah); *kuruma* (kuu-rue-mah)

Whose car is this?

Kore wa donata no jidōsha desu ka?
(koe-ray wah doe-nah-tah no jee-doe-shah dess kah)

automobile company – *jidōsha gaisha* (jee-doe-shah guy-shah)

I work for an automobile company.

Watashi wa jidōsha gaisha de hataraite imasu.
(wah-tah-she wah jee-doe-shah guy-shah day hah-tah-rye-tay ee-mahss)

auto parts – *jidōsha buhin* (jee-doe-shah buu-heen)

average – *heikin* (hay-keen)

What is the average price?

Heikin no nedan wa ikura desu ka?
(hay-keen no nay-dahn wah ee-kuu-rah dess kah)

average cost – *heikin genka* (hay-keen gen-kah)
average life – *heikin jumyō* (hay-keen juu-m'yoe)
average price – *heikin nedan* (hay-keen nay-dahn)
average unit cost – *heikin tanka* (hay-keen tahn-kah)
averaging – *heikin hō* (hay-keen hoe)
avoidable costs – *kaihi kanō genka* (kye-he kah-no gen-kah)

— B —

backdate – *mae hizuke ni suru* (my he-zuu-kay nee
  sue-rue)
  Can you backdate this?
    Kore wo mae hizuke ni suru koto ga dekimasu ka?
    (koe-ray oh my he-zuu-kay nee sue-rue koe-toe gah
    day-kee-mahss kah)
backlog – *chūmon zandaka* (chew-moan zahn-dah-
  kah)
  We have a large number of backlog orders.
    Takusan chumon zandaka ga arimasu.
    (tock-sahn chew-moan zahn-dah-kah gah ah-ree-
    mahss)
backlog of orders – *juchū daka* (juu-chew dah-kah)
back order – *mi chōtatsu chūmon* (me choe-tot-sue
  chew-moan)
back taxes – *sokyū kazei* (so-cue kah-zay)
bad business period – *fukeiki* (fuu-kay-kee)
  Business was bad in August.
    Hachigatsu wa fukeiki deshita.
    (hah-chee-got-sue wah fuu-kay-kee desh-tah)
bad check – *fuwatari kogitte* (fuu-wah-tah-ree koe-
  gheet-tay)
bad debt – *furyō saiken* (fuu-rio sigh-ken)
balance of payments – *kokusai shūshi* (coke-sigh
  shuu-she)
balance of trade – *bōeki shūshi* (boe-ay-kee shuu-she)
balance sheet – *taishaku taishō hyō* (tie-shah-kuu tie-
  show h'yoe)
balloon payment – *zangaku kijitsu ikkatsu hensai*
  (zahn-gah-kuu kee-jee-t'sue ee-cot-sue hen-sigh)
bank – *ginkō* (gheen-koe)

Please cash this at a bank.
Kore oh ginkō de genkin ni shite kudasai.
(koe-ray oh gheen-koe day gen-keen nee shtay kuu-dah-sigh)

bank acceptance – *ginkō hikiuke tegata* (gheen-koe he-kee-uu-kay tay-gah-tah)

bank account – *ginkō yokin kōza* (gheen-koe yoe-keen koe-zah)

bank balance – *ginkō yokin zandaka* (gheen-koe yoe-keen zahn-dah-kah)

bankbook – *tsūchō* (t'sue-choe)
Don't forget your bankbook.
Tsūchō wo wasurenaide.
(t'sue-choe oh wah-sue-ray-nigh-day)

bank charges – *ginkō tesūryō* (gheen-koe tay-sue-rio)

bank check – *ginkō kogitte* (gheen-koe koe-gheet-tay)

bank clerk – *ginkō-in* (gheen-koe-een)
Excuse me. Are you a bank clerk?
Shitsurei desu ga. Anata wa ginkō in desu ka?
(sheet-sue ray dess gah ah-nah-tah wah gheen-koe een dess kah)

bank deposit – *ginkō yokin* (gheen-koe yoe-keen)

bank draft – *ginkō tegata* (gheen-koe tay-gah-tah); foreign exchange bank draft – *gaikoku kawase tegata* (kah-wah-say tay-gah-tah)

banker – *ginkōka* (gheen-koe-kah)

bank holiday – *ginkō kyūjitsu* (gheen-koe cue-jee-t'sue)

bank interest – *ginkō risoku* (gheen-koe ree-so-kuu)

bank letter of credit – *ginkō shinyō jō* (gheen-koe sheen-yoe joe)

bank loan – *ginkō kashitsuke* (gheen-koe kah-she-t'sue-kay)

bank money order – *ginkō sōkin tegata* (gheen-koe so-keen tay-gah-tah)

bank note – *shihei* (she-hay)
Bank of America – *Banku obu Amerika* (bahn-ku oh-buu ah-may-ree-kah)
Bank of Japan (BOJ) – *Nihon Ginkō* (nee-hone gheen-koe)
Bank of Tokyo – *Tōkyō Ginkō* (toe-k'yoe gheen-koe)
bank rate – *kōtei buai* (koe-tay buu-eye)
bankrupt – *hasan* (hah-sahn)
    I hear he went bankrupt.
        Kare wa hasan shita to kikimashita.
        (kah-ray wah hah-sahn shtah toe kee-kee-mahsh-tah)
bank statement – *ginkō kanjō hōkoku sho* (gheen-koe kahn-joe hoe-koe-kuu show)
bank transfer – *ginkō furikomi* (gheen-koe fuu-ree-koe-me)
    I would like to make a bank transfer.
        Ginkō furikomi wo shitai desu.
        (gheen-koe fuu-ree-koe-me oh she-tie dess)
bar – *baa* (baah)
    Do you know any good bars not too far from the station?
        Eki no chikaku no ii baa wo shitte imasu ka?
        (ay-kee no chee-kah-kuu nee ee baah oh shtay ee-mahss kah)
bar chart – *bō gurafu* (boe guu-rah-fuu)
bareboat charter – *hadaka yōsen* (hah-dah-kah yoe-sen)
bargain – *kakuyasu hin* (kah-kuu-yah-sue heen)
bargaining power – *kōshō ken* (koe-show ken)
bargain securities – *baibai yakutei* (by-by yah-kuu-tay)
barter – *butsu-butsu kōkan* (boot-sue-boot-sue koe-kahn)
    China does a lot of bartering.

Chūgoku wa takusan butsu-butsu kōkan wo shite imasu.

(chew-go-kuu wah tock-sahn boot-sue-boot-sue koe-kahn oh shtay ee-mahss)

base currency – *kijun tsūka* (kee-june t'sue-kah)

base point – *kijun pointo* (kee-june point-oh)

base price – *kijun nedan* (kee-june nay-dahn)

base rate – *bēsu rēto* (bay-sue ray-toe)

base transportation rate – *ippan unchin ritsu* (eep-pahn uun-cheen ree-t'sue)

basic unit – *hontai* (hone-tie)
How much is the basic unit?
Hontai wa ikura desu ka?
(hone-tie wa ee-kuu-rah dess kah)

base year – *kijun nenji* (kee-june nen-jee)

batch processing – *ikkatsu shori* (ee-kah-t'sue show-ree)

batch production – *renzoku seisan* (ren-zoe-kuu say-sahn)

battery – *denchi* (den-chee); *batteri* (bah-tay-ree)
Your batteries are weak. You need new ones.
Denchi ga yowai desu. Atarashii no ga hitsuyō desu.
(den-chee gah yoe-why dess ah-tah-rah-she no gah he-t'sue-yoe dess)

baud – *bō* (boe)

bearer – *jisan nin* (jee-sahn neen)

bearer bond – *muki-mei saiken* (muu-kee-may sigh-ken)

bearer security – *muki-mei shōken* (muu-kee-may show-ken)

bear market – *uri sōba* (uu-ree so-bah)

beat-around-the-bush – *mawari kudoku* (mah-wah-ree kuu-doe-kuu)

become clear – *hakkiri suru* (hock-kee-ree sue-rue)
I understand clearly.

Hakkiri wakarimashita.
(hock-kee-ree wah-kah-ree-mahsh-tah)

behind the scenes talks – *nemawashi* (nay-mah-wah-she)

bell-shaped curve – *shōkei kyokusen* (show-kay k'yoe-kuu-sen)

"belly art" – *hara gei* (hah-rah gay)
The "art of the belly" is important when doing business in Japan.
Nihon de bijinesu wo suru toki hara gei ga taisetsu desu.
(nee-hone day bee-jee-ness oh sue-rue toe-kee hah-rah gay wah tie-say-t'sue dess)

below par – *gakumen ika de* (gah-kuu-men ee-kah day)

below-the-line item – *kakusen ka-no kōmoku* (kah-kuu-sen kah-no koe-moe-kuu)

beneficiary – *uketori nin* (uu-kay-toe-ree neen)

berth terms – *sennai ninpu chin senshu futan* (sen-nigh neen-puu cheen sen-shuu fuu-tahn)

bid for takeover – *kabushiki kaitori kōkai mōshikomi* (kah-buu-she-kee kye-toe-ree moe-she-koe-me)

big success – *dai seikō* (dye say-koe)
The project was a big success.
Purojekuto wa dai seikō shimashita.
(puu-roe-jeck-toe wah dye say-koe she-mahsh-tah)

bill (bank note) – *shihei* (she-hay)

bill (for purchases or sales) – *seikyū-sho* (say-cue-show)

bill (law) – *hōan* (hoe-ahn); **bill** (legislative) – *an* (ahn)
The bill is now in the Diet.
Hōan wa ima Gikai ni jōtei chū desu.
(hoe-ahn wah ee-mah ghee-kye nee joe-tay chew dess)

billboard – *keiji ban* (kay-jee bahn)

billion – *jū oku* (juu oh-kuu)

How much is one billion yen in dollars?

Dōru de jū oku en wa ikura desu ka?

(doe-rue day juu oh-kuu en wah ee-kuu-rah dess kah)

bill of exchange – *kawase tegata* (kah-wah-say tay-gah-tah)

Did you remember to bring the bill of exchange with you?

Kawase tegata wo wasurezu ni motte kimashita ka?

(kah-wah-say tay-gah-tah oh wah-sue-ray-zue nee moat-tay kee-mahsh-tah kah)

bill of lading – *funani shōken* (fuu-nah-nee show-ken)

Two copies of the bill of lading are necessary.

Funani shōken ga nibu irimasu.

(fuu-nah-nee show-ken gah nee-buu ee-ree-mahss)

bill of sale – *uriwatashi shōsho* (uu-ree-wah-tah-she show-show)

bill of sight – *kari yunyū negai* (kah-ree yuun-yuu nay-guy)

biochemistry – *seikagaku* (say-kah-gah-kuu)

bio-computer – *baio konpyūta* (bio comb-pew-tah)

birthday – *tanjōbi* (tahn-joe-bee)

When is your birthday?

O-tanjōbi wa itsu desu ka?

(oh-tahn-joe-bee wah eat-sue dess kah)

BIT (computer) – *bitto* (beet-toe)

black-and-white TV – *shiro kuro terebi* (she-roe kuu-roe tay-ray-bee)

black figure (showing a profit) – *kuro ji* (kuu-roe jee)

Last month we began showing a profit.

Sengetsu kuro ji ga demashita.

(sen-gate-sue kuu-roe jee gah day-mahsh-tah)

black market – *yami ichiba* (yah-me ee-chee-bah); *burakku māketto* (buu-rahk-kuu mah-kate-toe)

blanket order – *sōkatsu chūmon* (so-kah-t'sue chew-moan)

blanket order for production – *keizoku seizō sashizu-sho* (kay-zoe-kuu say-zoe sah-she-zuu-show)

bleed (an advertisement that covers the entire page) – *tachikiri* (tah-chee-kee-ree)

blockage of funds – *shikin fūsa* (she-keen fuu-sah)

blocked currency – *fūsa tsūka* (fuu-sah t'sue-kah)

blowup (enlarge a photograph or piece of art) – *hikinobashi* (he-kee-no-bah-she)

blue-chip stock – *yūryō kabu* (yuu-rio kah-buu)

blue-collar worker – *rōdōsha* (roe-doe-shah); *burū karā* (buu-rue kah-rah)

blueprint – *ao jashin* (ah-oh jah-sheen)

board meeting – *torishimariyaku kaigi* (toe-ree-she-mah-ree-yah-kuu kye-ghee)

board of directors – *riji kai* (ree-jee kye)
He is holding a meeting of the board of directors.
Riji kai no kaigi wo yatte imasu.
(ree-jee kye no kye-ghee oh yaht-tay ee-mahss)

boardroom – *kaigi shitsu* (kye-ghee sheet-sue)

body (of vehicle) – *shatai* (shah-tie)

boilerplate contract – *keiyaku sho ni fukumareru hyōjun jōkō* (kay-yah-kuu show nee fuu-kuu-mah-ray-rue h'yoe-june joe-koe)

bond – *saiken* (sigh-ken)

bond areas – *hozei chiiki* (hoe-zay chee-ee-kee)

bonded carrier – *hozei kamotsu unpan nin* (hoe-zay kah-moat-sue uun-pahn neen)

bonded goods – *hozei kamotsu* (hoe-zay kah-moat-sue)

bond issue – *shasai hakkō* (sha-sigh hock-oh)

bond rating – *saiken kakuzuke* (sigh-ken kah-kuu-zuu-kay)

bonded warehouse – *hozei sōko* (hoe-zay so-koe)

bonus (premium) – *rieki haitō* (ree-ay-kee high-toe);
   bonuses paid to employees – *shōyo* (show-yoe);
   bōnasu (boe-nah-sue)

book inventory – *chōbo tana-oroshi* (choe-boe tah-
   nah-oh-roe-she)

bookkeeper – *chōbogakari* (choe-boe-gah-kah-ree)

bookkeeping – *boki* (boe-kee)

book value – *chōbo kakaku* (choe-boe kah-kah-kuu)

book value per share – *hitokabu atari no chōbo*
   kakaku (shtoe-kah-buu ah-tah-ree no choe-boe kah-
   kah-kuu)

boom (business) – *kōkyō* (koe-k'yoe); *būmu* (buu-muu);
   niwaka keiki (nee-wah-kah kay-kee)

border (between countries) – *kokkyō* (coke-yoe)
   The factory is right next to the border.
     Kōjō wa kokkyō no sugu soba desu.
     (koe-joe wah coke-yoe no sue-guu so-bah dess)

border-tax adjustment – *kokkyō zei chōsei* (coke-yoe
   zay choe-say)

borrow – *kariru* (kah-ree-rue); take out a loan – *shak-*
   kin suru (shahk-keen sue-rue)
   May I borrow your tool box?
     Dōgu bako wo karite mo ii desu ka?
     (doe-guu bah-koe oh kah-ree-tay moe ee dess kah)

boss – *jōshi* (joe-she)

bottom price – *soko ne* (so-koe nay)
   Is that your bottom price?
     Sore wa soko ne desu ka?
     (so-ray wah so-koe nay dess kah)

boycott – *boikotto suru* (boy-cot-toe sue-rue)

brainstorm – *burein sutōmu* (buu-ray-een stow-muu)

brake (on vehicle) – *burēki* (buu-ray-kee)

branch (sub-division) – *shibu* (she-buu)
   Are you a sub-division of that company?
     Sono kaisha no shibu no kata desu ka?

(so-no kye-shah no she-buu no kah-tah dess kah)

branch manager – *shiten chō* (she-ten choe)

He is the new branch manager.

Kare wa atarashii shiten chō desu.

(kah-ray wah ah-tah-rah-she she-ten choe dess)

branch office (store) – *shiten* (she-ten)

Next year I will move to a branch office.

Rainen shiten ni utsurimasu.

(rye-nen she-ten nee uu-t'sue-ree-mahss)

brand – *meigara* (may-gah-rah); *burando* (buu-rahn-doe)

brand acceptance – *meigara shōnin* (may-gah-rah show-neen)

brand image – *meigara imēji* (may-gah-rah ee-may-jee); *shōhyō imēji* (show-h'yoe ee-may-jee)

brand loyalty – *meigara chūjitsu-sei* (may-gah-rah chew-jee-t'sue-say)

brand name – *meikā hin* (may-kah heen)

brand recognition – *meigara ninshiki* (may-gah-rah neen-she-kee)

break (rest from work) – *kyūkei* (cue-kay)

Everyone is on break.

Minna kyūkei shiteimasu.

(mean-nah cue-kay shtay-mahss)

break even – *son'eki nashi ni naru* (so-nay-kee nah-she nee nah-rue)

break-even analysis – *son'eki bunki-ten bunseki* (so-nay-kee boon-kee-ten boon-say-kee)

break-even point – *son'eki bunki-ten* (so-nay-kee boon-kee-ten)

break-up (dissolution) – *kaisan* (kye-sahn)

Unfortunately, that company was dissolved.

Ainiku, sono kaisha wa kaisan shimashita.

(eye-nee-kuu so-no kye-shah wah kye-sahn she-mahsh-tah)

bribery – *baishū* (by-shuu)
   He was connected with a bribery case three years
   ago.
      *San nen mae ni kare wa baishū no kēsu ni kankei
      ga arimashita.*
      (sahn nen my nee kah-ray wah buy-shuu no kay-
      sue nee kahn-kay gah ah-ree-mahsh-tah)
briefcase – *buriifu kēsu* (buu-ree-fuu kay-sue); *kaban*
   (kah-bahn)
British Embassy – *Eikoku Taishikan* (ay-koe-kuu tie-
   she-kahn)
brochure – *panfuretto* (pahn-fuu-rate-toe)
   Please let me see the brochure.
      Panfuretto wo misete kudasai.
      (pan-fuu-rate-toe oh me-say-tay kuu-dah-sigh)
broken lot – *hakabu* (hah-kah-buu)
broker – *nakagainin* (nah-kah-guy-neen); *burōkā*
   (buu-roe-kah)
budget – *yosan* (yoe-sahn)
budget appropriation – *yosan wariate* (yoe-sahn
   wah-ree-ah-tay)
budget forecast – *yosan yosoku* (yoe-sahn yoe-so-kuu)
buffer memory – *baffā memorii* (bah-fah may-more-
   ree)
bull market – *kai sōba* (kye so-bah)
bumper (of vehicle) – *banpa* (bahn-pah)
burden (obligation) – *futan* (fuu-tahn)
   That much rent is a heavy burden.
      Sonna ni takai yachin wa omoi futan desu.
      (soan-nah nee tah-kye yah-cheen wah oh-moy fuu-
      tahn dess)
bureaucracy (bureaucrat) – *kanryō* (kahn-rio)
bureaucrat – *kanryō sha* (kahn-rio shah)
   He is one hundred percent bureaucrat.
      Kare wa hyaku pāsento no kanryō sha desu.

(kah-ray wah h'yah-kuu pah-sen-toe no kahn-rio
sha dess)

bureau director – *kyoku chō* (k'yoe-kuu choe)
Mr. Sato was promoted to bureau director.
Sato-san wa kyoku chō ni shōshin saremashita.
(sah-toe-sahn wah k'yoe-kuu choe nee show-sheen
sah-ray-mahsh-tah)

business (occupation) – *shokugyō* (show-kuu-g'yoe)
What is Mr. Green's business?
Gurīn-san no shokugyō wa nan desu ka?
(guu-reen-sahn no show-kuu-g'yoe wah nahn des
kah)

business (as in asking someone why they are visiting
an office) – *yōken* (yoe-ken); have business with someone – *yōji ga aru* (yoe-jee gah ah-rue)
What is your business (may I help you)?
Gō-yoken wa?
(go-yoe-ken wah)
I have business with Mr. Yamamoto.
Yamamoto-san ni yōji ga arimasu.
(yah-mah-moe-toe-sahn nee yoe-jee gah ah-ree-
mahss)

business (trade) – *eigyō* (ay-g'yoe); *jigyō* (jee-g'yoe);
business results – *jigyō naiyō* (jee-g'yoe nigh-yoe)
Is this a new business?
Kore wa atarashii jigyō desu ka?
(koe-ray wah ah-tah-rah-she jee-g'yoe dess kah)

business activity – *keiki* (kay-kee)

business affairs section – *gyōmu* (g'yoe-muu)
Mr. Mochizuki is in the business affairs section.
Mochizuki-san wa gyōmu bu ni imasu.
(moe-chee-zuu-kee-sahn wah g'yoe-muu buu nee ee-
mahss)

business area – *shōgyō chiku* (show-g'yoe chee-kuu)
Is Hokkaido one of your business areas?

Hokkaidō wa anata no shōgyō chiku no hitotsu
desu ka?

(hoe-kye-doe wah ah-nah-tah no show-g'yoe chee-
kuu no he-tote-sue dess kah)

business card – *meishi* (may-she)

Have I already received your business card?

O-meishi mō chodai shita deshō ka?

(oh-may-she moe choe-dye shtah day-show kah)

Where can I have cards made?

Doko de meishi wa tsukuremasu ka?

(doe-koe day may-she wah t'sue-kuu-ray-mahss
kah)

business cycle – *keiki junkan* (kay-kee june-kahn)

business development mission – *shōbai seichō no*
shisetsu (show-by say-choe no she-say-t'sue)

business hours – *eigyō jikan* (ay-g'yoe jee-kahn)

What are that shop's business hours?

Sono mise no eigyō jikan wa nanji kara nanji made
desu ka?

(so-no me-say no ay-g'yoe jee-kahn wah nan-jee
kah-rah nan-jee mah-day dess kah)

businessman – *gyōsha* (g'yoe-shah)

All of the guests are businessmen.

O-kyakusan wa minna gyōsha desu.

(oh-k'yack-sahn wah mean-nah g'yoe-shah dess)

business management – *keiei kanri* (kay-ay kahn-
ree)

business meeting – *kaigō* (kye-go)

business partner – *torihiki saki* (toe-ree-he-kee sah-
kee)

This is my business partner.

Kono kata wa watakushi no torihiki saki no kata
desu.

(koe-no kah-tah wah wah-tock-she no toe-ree-he-
kee sah-kee no kah-tah dess)

business plan – *keiei kanri keikaku* (kay-ay kahn-ree kay-kah-kuu)

business policy – *keiei hōshin* (kay-ay hoe-sheen)

business practices – *shōshūkan* (show-shuu-kahn)
> You must learn new business practices.
>> *Atarashii shōshūkan wo manabu beki desu.*
>> (ah-tah-rah-she show-shuu-kahn oh mah-nah-buu bay-kee dess)

business report – *eigyō hōkokusho* (ay-g'yoe hoe-koe-kuu-show)

business strategy – *keiei senryaku* (kay-ay sen-rah-kuu)

business tie-up – *kigyō teiki* (kee-g'yoe tay-kee)

business transaction – *torihiki* (toe-ree-he-kee)

business trip – *shutchō* (shuu-choe)
> Mr. Lee is away on a business trip.
>> *Ree-san wa shutchō shiteimasu.*
>> (ree-sahn wah shuu-choe shtay-mahss)

business world – *gyōkai* (g'yoe-kye)
> Japan's business world is very interesting.
>> *Nihon no gyōkai wa taihen omoshiroi desu.*
>> (nee-hone no g'yoe-kye wah tie-hen oh-moe-she-roy dess)

buy (purchase) – *kau* (cow)
> I'd like to buy this car.
>> *Kono jidōsha wo kaitai desu.*
>> (koe-no jee-doe-shah oh kye-tie dess)
> I bought it yesterday.
>> *Kinō kaimashita.*
>> (kee-no kye-mahsh-tah)
> Please buy this book for me.
>> *Kono hon wo watashi ni katte kudasai.*
>> (koe-no hone oh wah-tah-she nee kah-tay kuu-dah-sigh)

buy back – *kaimodosu* (kye-moe-doe-suu)

buyer – *kaite* (kye-tay)

buyer's market – *kaite shijō* (kye-tay she-joe)

buyer's option – *kaite-no sentaku-ken* (kye-tay-no sen-tah-kuu-ken)

buyer's responsibility – *kaite-gawa sekinin* (kye-tay-gah-wah say-kee-neen)

buy on close – *ōbike de kau* (oh-bee-kay day cow)

buy on opening – *yoritsuki de kau* (yoe-ree-t'sue-kee day cow)

buy-out – *baishū* (by-shuu)

bylaws – *teikan* (tay-kahn)

by-product – *fuku-sanbutsu* (fuu-kuu-sahn-boot-sue)

— C —

cabaret – *kyabarē* (k'yah-bah-ray)*
  *This is the official designation for Japan's famous
  hostess clubs.
  Let's drop in to a cabaret tonight before returning to
  the hotel.
  *Konban hoteru ni kaeru mae ni kyabarē ni
  yorimashō.*
  (comb-bahn hoe-tay-rue nee kye-rue my nee k'yah-
  bah-ray nee yoe-ree-mah-show)
cable – *denshin* (den-sheen)
cable transfer – *denshin sōkin* (den-sheen so-keen)
calculator – *keisanki* (kay-sahn-kee)
  Do you have a calculator?
  Keisanki wo motte imasu ka?
  (kay-sahn-kee oh moat-tay ee-mahss kah)
call-back (product recall) – *kaishū* (kye-shuu)
call-loan – *kōru rōn* (koe-rue roan)
call on; visit – *tazuneru* (tah-zuu-nay-rue); *hōmon
  suru* (hoe-moan sue-rue)
  I want to visit Mr. Watanabe tomorrow.
  Ashita Watanabe-san wo o-tazune shitai desu.
  (ah-shtah wah-tah-nah-bay-sahn oh oh-tah-zuu-
  nay she-tie dess)
Canadian Embassy –*Kanada Taishikan* (kah-nah-
  dah tie-she-kahn)
cancel – *torikesu* (toe-ree-kay-sue); *kaishō suru* (kye-
  show sue-rue)
  Please cancel my reservations.
  Watashi no yoyaku wo torikeshite kudasai.
  (wah-tock-she no yoe-yah-kuu oh toe-ree-kay-shtay
  kuu-dah-sigh)

That flight has been canceled.
Sono bin wa torikesaremashita.
(so-no bean wah toe-ree-kay-sah-ray-mahsh-tah)

canceled check – *masshō kogitte* (mah-show koe-gheet-tay)

cancellation charge – *torikeshi ryō* (toe-ree-kay-she rio)

capacity – *nōryoku* (no-rio-kuu)

capital (money) – *shihon kin* (she-hone keen)
How much capital is needed to start a new company in Japan?
Nihon de atarashii kaisha wo tsukuru tame ni shihon kin wa dono gurai hitsuyō desu ka?
(nee-hone day ah-tah-rah-she kye-shah oh t'sue-kuu-rue tah-may nee she-hone keen wah doe-no guu-rye heat-sue-yoe dess kah)

capital account – *shihon kanjō* (she-hone kahn-joe)

capital allowance – *shihon hikiate* (she-hone he-kee-ah-tay)

capital asset – *kotei shisan* (koe-tay she-sahn)

capital expenditure – *shihon shishutsu* (she-hone she-shoot-sue)

capital exports – *shihon yushutsu* (she-hone yuu-shoot-sue)

capital formation – *shihon keisei* (she-hone kay-say)

capital gain/loss – *shihon ritoku oyobi sonshitsu* (she-hone ree-toe-kuu oh-yoe-bee soan-sheet-sue)

capital goods – *shihon zai* (she-hone zye)

capital increase – *shihon zōka* (she-hone zoe-kah)

capital intensive – *shihon shūyaku* (she-hone shuu-yah-kuu)

capitalism – *shihon shugi* (she-hone shuu-ghee)
Capitalism is now very popular in China.
Chūgoku de shihon shugi wa taihen ninki ga arimasu.

(chew-go-kuu day she-hone shuu-ghee wah tie-hen neen-kee gah ah-ree-mahss)

capitalization – *shihon-ka* (she-hone-kah)

capital market – *shihon shijō* (she-hone she-joe)

capital spending – *shihon shishutsu* (she-hone she-shoot-sue)

capital stock – *kabushiki shihon kin* (kah-buu-she-kee she-hone keen)

capital structure – *shihon kōsei* (she-hone koe-say)

capital surplus – *shihon jōyo kin* (she-hone joe-yoe keen)

capsule – *kapuseru* (kahp-say-rue)

car – *jidōsha* (jee-doe-shah); *kuruma* (kuu-rue-mah)

cargo; freight – *kamotsu* (kah-moat-sue); *tsumini* (t'sue-me-nee)

How much do you think the freight charge will be?

Kamotsu ryō wa ikura ni naru to omoimasu ka?

(kah-moat-sue rio wah ee-kuu-rah nee nah-rue toe oh-moe-ee-mahss kah)

carload – *issha kashikiri kamotsu* (eesh-shah kah-she-kee-ree kah-moat-sue)

carrier – *unsō gyōsha* (uun-so g'yoe-shah)

carrier's risk – *unsō gyōsha kiken tanpo* (uun-so g'yoe-shah kee-ken tahn-poe)

carry (transport) – *hakobu* (hah-koe-buu); carry out, put into practice – *jikkō suru* (jeek-koe sue-rue)

The goods have already been transported to the warehouse.

Shinamono wa mō sōko ni hakobaremashita.

(she-nah-moe-no wah moh so-koh nee hah-koe-bah-ray-mahsh-tah)

carry-back – *kurimodoshi* (kuu-ree-moe-doe-she)

carry forward – *susumeru* (sue-sue-may-rue)

carry forward accounting – *kurikosu* (kuu-ree-koe-sue)

carrying charges – *shogakari* (show-gah-kah-ree)

carry-over (accounting) – *kurikoshi* (kuu-ree-koe-she)

carry-over merchandise – *zanpin* (zahn-peen)

cartel – *kigyō rengō* (kee-g'yoe ren-go); *karuteru* (kah-rue-tay-rue)

car telephone – *jidōsha denwa* (jee-doe-shah den-wah)

case (in case) – *baai* (bah-eye)

In that case, I will go to Tokyo next week.
> *Sono baai niwa watakushi wa raishū Tōkyō e ikimasu.*
> (so-no bah-eye nee-wah wah-tock-she wah rye-shuu toe-k'yoe ay ee-kee-mahss)

cash – *genkin* (gen-keen)

Please pay in cash.
> *Genkin de haratte kudasai.*
> (gen-keen day hah-rah-tay kuu-dah-sigh)

cash-and-carry – *genkin tentō watashi no* (gen-keen ten-toe wah-tah-she no)

cash-and-carry (trade) – *genkin jikokusen shugi no* (gen-keen jee-koe-kuu-sen shu-ghee no)

cash balance – *genkin zandaka* (gen-keen zahn-dah-kah)

cash basis – *genkin bēsu* (gen-keen bay-sue)

cash basis (accounting) – *genkin shugi* (gen-keen shuu-ghee)

cash before delivery – *hikiwatashi mae no genkin barai* (he-kee-wah-tah-she my no gen-keen bah-rye)

cash book – *genkin suitō-bo* (gen-keen sue-ee-toe-boe)

cash budget – *genkin shūshi yosan* (gen-keen shuu-she yoe-sahn)

cash delivery – *tōjitsu kessai torihiki* (toe-jee-t'sue case-sigh toe-ree-he-kee)

cash discount – *genkin waribiki* (gen-keen wah-ree-bee-kee)

cash dividend – *genkin haitō* (gen-keen high-toe)

cash entry – *futsū yunyū shinkoku* (fuu-t'sue yuun-yuu sheen-koe-kuu)

cash flow – *genkin ryūdō* (gen-keen r'yuu-doe)

cashier – *suitō gakari* (sue-ee-toe gah-kah-ree); *genkin gakari* (gen-keen gah-kah-ree); cashier in restaurant or store – *kaikei* (kye-kay)
Please take it to the cashier (in bank).
Genkin gakari ni motte itte kudasai.
(gen-keen gah-kah-ree nee moat-tay eat-tay kuu-dah-sigh)

cashier's check – *shiharainin kogitte* (she-hah-rye-neen koe-gheet-tay)

cash-in-advance – *mae-barai* (my-bah-rye)

cash-on-delivery – *genkin hikikae-barai* (gen-keen he-kee-kye-bah-rye)

cash register – *rejisuta* (ray-jees-tah)

cassette – *kasetto* (kah-set-toe)

casual – *fui-no* (fuu-ee-no); *kudaketa* (kuu-dah-kay-tah)
Will casual clothing be all right for tonight's party?
Konban no pātii niwa kudaketa yōfuku de yoroshii desu ka?
(comb-bahn no pah-tee nee-wah kuu-dah-kay-tah yoe-fuu-kuu day yoe-roe-she dess kah)

casualty insurance – *saigai hoken* (sigh-guy hoe-ken)

catalog – *katarogu* (kah-tah-roe-guu)

catalyst – *shokubai* (show-kuu-by)

category (kinds) – *shurui* (shuu-rue-ee)
We have two kinds of imported merchandise.
Yunyūhin wa ni shurui arimasu.
(yuun-yuu heen wah nee shuu-rue-ee ah-ree-mahss)

cause – *gen'in* (gen-een)
Do you know the cause of the problem?

Sono mondai no gen'in wo gozonji desu ka?
(so-no moan-dye no gain-een oh go-zone-jee dess kah)

cause trouble (inconvenience) – *meiwaku wo kakeru* (may-wah-kuu oh kah-kay-rue)

I do not want to cause anybody any trouble.
Dare ni mo meiwaku wo kaketaku nai no desu.
(dah-ray nee moe may-wah-kuu oh kah-kay-tah-kuu nigh no dess)

CB radio – *shimin rajio* (she-mean rah-jee-oh)

ceiling – *saikō gendo* (sigh-koe gen-doe)

Central Bank – *Chūō Ginkō* (chew-oh gheen-koe)

centralization – *shūchū-ka* (shuu-chew-kah)

central rate – *sentoraru rēto* (sen-toe-rah-rue ray-toe)

certificate – *shōmei sho* (show-may show)

All overseas shipments must have a certificate.
Subete no kaigai no tsumini wah shōmeisho ga hitsuyō desu.
(sue-bay-tay no kye-guy no t'sue-me-nee wah show-may-show ga sheet-sue-yoe dess)

certificate (securities) – *shōken* (show-ken)

certificate of deposit – *yokin shōsho* (yoe-keen show-show)

certificate of incorporation – *kaisha setsuritsu kyoka-shō* (kye-shah say-t'sue-ree-t'sue k'yoe-kah-show)

certificate of origin – *gensanchi shōmei sho* (gen-sahn-chee show-may-show)

certified check – *hoshō kogitte* (hoe-show koe-ghee-tay)

certified public accountant – *kōnin kaikeishi* (koe-neen kye-kay-she)

certify – *shōmei suru* (show-may sue-rue)

chain of command – *shiki keitō* (she-kee kay-toe)

chain store – *chēn sutoa* (chain stow-ah)

chain store group – *chēn sutoa soshiki* (chain stow-ah so-she-kee)

chairman of the board – *torishimariyaku kaichō* (toe-ree-she-mah-ree-yah-kuu kye-choe); *kaichō* (kye-choe)

This proposal must go to the chairman of the board.
Kono ringi sho wa kaichō ni mawasanakereba nar-anai.
(koe-no reen-ghee-show wah kye-choe nee mah-wah-sah-nah-kay-ray-bah nah-rah-nigh)

chairman of a conference – *gichō* (ghee-choe)

challenge – *chōsen* (choe-sen); serious challenge – *shinken na chōsen* (sheen-ken nah choe-sen)

Your project is a very interesting challenge.
Anata no purojekuto wa taihen omoshiroi chōsen desu.
(ah-nah-tah no puu-roe-jake-toe wah tie-hen oh-moe-she-roy choe-sen dess)

Chamber of Commerce and Industry – *Shō Kō Kaigi Sho* (show koe kye-ghee show)

change (amend) – *henkō* (hen-koe)

If you will amend this contract I will sign it.
Kono keiyaku wo henkō sureba shomei shimasu.
(koe-no kay-yah-kuu oh hen-koe sue-ray-bah show-may she-mahss)

change (money back) – *otsuri* (oh-t'sue-ree)

I forgot my change.
Otsuri wo wasuremashita.
(oh-t'sue-ree oh wah-sue-ray-mah-shtah)

change (small coins for telephone, etc.) – *komakai okane* (koe-mah-kye oh-kah-nay); to change a bill – *kuzusu* (kuu-zuu-sue)

Please change this bill (into small money).
Kono o-satsu wo kuzushite kudasai.

(koe-no oh-sah-t'sue oh kuu-zuu-shtay kuu-dah-
    sigh)

channel of distribution – *ryūtsū keiro* (ree-uu-t'sue
    kay-roe)

charge account – *urikake-kin kanjō* (uu-ree-kah-kay-
    keen kahn-joe)

charter (for shipping) – *yōsen* (yoe-sen); charter (a
    boat, etc.) – *kashikiri* (kah-she-kee-ree)

chartered accountant – *kōnin kaikeishi* (koe-neen
    kye-kay-she)

chassis (of automobile) – *shashi* (shah-she)

chattel – *dōsan* (doe-sahn)

chattel mortgage – *dōsan teitō* (doe-sahn tay-toe)

cheap – *yasui* (yah-sue-ee); cheaper – *motto yasui*
    (moat-toe yah-sue-ee); cheapest – *ichiban yasui* (ee-
    chee-bahn yah-sue-ee)

check (bank) – *kogitte* (koe-gheet-tay)
    I will mail you a check tomorrow.
       Ashita yūbin de kogitte wo okurimasu.
       (ah-shtah yuu-bean nee koe-ghee-tay oh oh-kuu-
       ree-mahss)

check (investigate) – *shiraberu* (she-rah-bay-rue)
    It is very important to check out a company before
    doing business with it.
       *Torihiki suru mae ni kaisha wo shiraberu no wa
       jūdai na koto desu.*
       (toe-ree-he-kee sue-rue my nee kye-shah oh she-
       rah-bay-rue no wah juu-dye nah koe-toe dess)

checking account – *tōza yokin kōza* (toe-zah yoe-
    keen koe-zah)

    I have a checking account in the Yurakucho branch
    of the Mitsubishi Bank.
       *Watashi wa Mitsubishi Ginkō no Yūrakuchō shiten
       ni tōza yokin kōza wo motte imasu.*

(wah-tah-she wah meet-sue-bee-she gheen-koe no
yuu-rah-kuu-choe she-ten nee toe-zah yoe-keen koe-
zah oh moat-tay ee-mahss)

checklist – *shōgō hyō* (show-go h'yoe)

chemical (product) – *kagaku seihin* (kah-gah-kuu say-
heen)

chief accountant – *kaikei shunin* (kye-kay shuu-neen)

chief buyer – *kōbai shunin* (koe-buy shuu-neen)

chief executive – *saikō keiei sekinin sha* (sigh-koe
kay-ay no say-kee-neen shah)

Chinese food – *chūka ryōri* (chew-kah rio-ree)

chip (computer) – *chippu* (cheap-puu)

chopsticks – *o-hashi* (oh-hah-she); splittable wooden
chopsticks joined at one end – *waribashi* (wah-ree-
bah-she)

circuit breaker – *kairo shadanki* (kye-roe shah-dahn-
kee)

circumstance – *jijō* (jee-joe)
  These circumstances are very serious. Can you explain
  them?
  *Kono jijō wa taihen shinkoku desu. Setsumei
  dekimasu ka?*
  (koe-no jee-joe wah tie-hen sheen-koe-kuu dess say-
  t'sue-may day-kee-mahss kah)

civil engineer – *doboku kōgaku sha* (doe-boe-kuu koe-
gah-kuu shah)

claim (request) – *seikyū suru* (say-cue sue-rue);
kūrēmu (kuu-ray-muu)
  I would like to make a claim regarding this shipment.
  Kono tsumini ni kūrēmu wo tsuketai desu.
  (koe-no t'sue-me-nee nee kuu-ray-muu oh t'sue-kay-
  tie dess)

claim (for business loss) – *songai baishō seikyū* (soan-
guy buy-show say-cue)

claim (for insurance) – *shiharai seikyū* (she-hah-rye say-cue)

classified ad – *kōmoku-betsu kōkoku* (koe-moe-kuu-bait-sue koe-koe-kuu)

classmate – *dōkyūsei* (doe-cue-say)
They are classmates.
    Ano hito-tachi wa dōkyūsei desu.
    (ah-no shtoe-tah-chee wah doe-cue-say dess)

clearinghouse – *tegata kōkansho* (tay-gah-tah koe-khan-show)

clerk in office – *jimu in* (jee-muu een); clerk in bank – *ginkō in* (gheen-koe een); clerk in shop – *ten in* (ten een)

client – *irainin* (ee-rye-neen); *o-kyaku-san* (oh-kyack-sahn)

climate – *kikō* (kee-koe)

closed account – *fūsa kanjō* (fuu-sah kahn-joe)

closely held corporation – *hi-kōkai gaisha* (he-koe-kye guy-shah)

closing entry – *kessan kin'yū* (case-sahn keen-yuu)

closing price – *ōbike nedan* (oh-bee-kay nay-dahn)

closing time of door, gate – *mon gen* (moan gen)

clutch – *kuratchi* (kuu-rah-chee)

coffee break – *kyūkei jikan* (cue-kay jee-kahn)

collateral – *mikaeri tanpo* (me-kye-ree tahn-poe)

colleague – *dōryō* (doe-rio)

collect-call – *senpō barai* (sem-poe bah-rye)
I would like to make a collect call to Chicago.
    Shikago ni senpō barai denwa wo kaketai no desu.
    (she-kah-go nee sem-poe bah-rye den-wah oh kah-kay-tie no dess)

collect information – *shuzai suru* (shuu-zye sue-rue)
She has gone to Tokyo to collect information for a magazine article.

Kanojo wa zasshi no kiji no tame ni Tōkyō e shuzai ni ikimashita.

(kah-no-joe wah zah-she no kee-jee no tah-may nee toe-k'yoe ay shuu-zye nee ee-kee-mahsh-tah)

collection period – *toritate kikan* (toe-ree-tah-tay kee-kahn)

collective agreement – *dantai kyōyaku* (dahn-tie k'yoe-yah-kuu)

collective bargaining – *dantai kōshō* (dahn-tie koe-show)

collect on delivery – *daikin hikikae barai* (dye-keen he-kee-kye bah-rye)

color – *iro* (ee-roe)

The color is wrong.

Iro ga chigaimasu.

(ee-roe gah chee-guy-mahss)

color TV – *karā terebi* (kah-rah tay-ray-bee)

commemorate – *kinen suru* (kee-nen sue-rue)

They want to commemorate the first year of our tie-up.

Teikei no dai-ichi nen wo kinen shitai desu.

(tay-kay no dye-ee-chee nen oh kee-nen she-tie dess)

commerce – *tsūshō* (t'sue-show)

commercial advertisement (TV) – *komāsharu* (koe-mah-shah-rue)

commercial attaché – *shomu kan* (show-muu kahn)

commercial bank – *shichū ginkō* (she-chew gheen-koe)

commercial grade – *shōgyō kakuzuke* (show-g'yoe kah-kuu-zuu-kay)

commercial invoice – *shōgyō okurijō* (show-g'yoe oh-kuu-ree-joe)

commission (fee) – *tesūryō* (tay-sue-rio)

commission agency – *toritsugi* (toe-ree-t'sue-ghee)

commitment – *yakutei* (yah-kuu-tay)

committee – *i-in-kai* (ee-een-kye)

Committee for Economic Development (an important business organization in Japan) – *Keizai Dōyūkai* (kay-zye doe-yuu-kye)

committee meeting – *i-in-kaigi* (ee-een-kye-ghee)

commodity – *shōhin* (show-heen)

commodity exchange – *shōhin torihikisho* (show-heen toe-ree-he-kee-show)

commodity tax – *buppin zei* (buu-peen zay)
  Does that include the commodity tax?
    Buppin zei mo haitte imasu ka?
    (buu-peen zay moe height-tay ee-mahss kah)

common carrier – *ippan unsō gyōsha* (eep-pahn uunso g'yoe-shah)

common market – *kyōdō shijō* (k'yoe-doe she-joe)

common stock – *futsū kabu* (fuu-t'sue kah-buu)

communication (correspondence) – *tsūshin* (t'sue-sheen)
  I would like to talk to your correspondence clerk.
    Tsūshin gakari ni hanashitai desu.
    (t'sue-sheen gah-kah-ree nee hah-nah-she-tie dess)

communism – *kyōsan shugi* (k'yoe-sahn shuu-ghee)

commuting allowance – *tsūkin teate* (t'sue-keen tay-ah-tay)
  Do you also receive a commuting allowance?
    Anata wa tsūkin teate mo moraimasu ka?
    (ah-nah-tah wah t'sue-keen tay-ah-tay mo moe-rye-mahss kah)

compact disc – *konpakuto disuku* (cone-pah-kuu-toe disk-uu)

compact disc player – *konpakuto disuku purēya* (cone-pah-kuu-toe disk-uu puu-ray-yah)

company – *kaisha* (kye-shah)

company employee – *kaishain* (kye-shah-een)

company expense, at – *kaisha mochi de* (kye-shah moe-chee day)

I went to Osaka last week at company expense.
  Senshū kaisha mochi de Ōsaka e ikimashita.
  (sen-shuu kye-shah moe-chee day oh-sah-kah ay ee-kee-mahsh-tah)

company goal – *kigyō mokuteki* (kee-g'yoe moe-kuu-tay-kee)

company owned by foreign interests – *gaishikei gaisha* (guy-she-kay guy-shah)

company pension – *kōsei nenkin* (koe-say nen-keen)

company policy – *kigyō seisaku* (kee-g'yoe say-sah-kuu)

company recreational trip – *ian ryokō* (ee-ahn rio-koe)

company union – *kigyōbetsu kumiai* (kee-g'yoe-bait-sue kuu-me-eye)

company villa (may also be private) – *bessō* (base-so)

company with limited liability – *yūgen gaisha* (yuu-gen guy-shah)

company with some foreign equity – *gaishikei kaisha* (guy-she-kay kye-shah)

compensation – *hōshū* (hoe-shuu)

compensation trade – *kyūshō bōeki* (cue-show boe-ay-kee)

competition – *kyōsō* (k'yoe-so)

There is no competition in this industry.
  Kono gyōkai ni kyōsō wa arimasen.
  (koe-no g'yoe-kye nee k'yoe-so gah ah-ree-mah-sen)

competitive advantage – *kyōsō jō no riten* (k'yoe-so jo no ree-ten); *sērusu pointo* – (say-rue-sue point-oh)

competitive edge – *kyōsō-jō no yūetsu-sei* (k'yoe-so joe-no yuu-ate-sue-say)

competitive price – *kyōsō nedan* (k'yoe-so nay-dahn)

competitive strategy – *kyōsō senryaku* (k'yoe-so sen-ree-yah-kuu)

competitor – *kyōsō aite* (k'yoe-so eye-tay)

competitor analysis – *kyōsō sha bunseki* (k'yoe-so shah boon-say-kee)

competitors (company) – *kyōsōsha* (k'yoe-so-shah)

complain – *kobosu* (koe-boe-sue); nothing to complain about – *kobosu koto wa nai* (koe-boe-sue koe-toe wah nigh); *fuhei wo iu* (fuu-hay oh yuu)

He is always complaining to me.
> *Ano hito wa watashi ni itsumo koboshite imasu.*
> (ah-no shtoe wah wah-tah-she nee eat-sue-moe koe-boe-shtay ee-mahss)

complaint (grievance) – *kujō* (kuu-joe); *kujō wo iu* (kuu-joe oh yuu)

What is your complaint this time?
> *Kondo no kujō wa nan desu ka?*
> (cone-doe no kuu-joe wah nahn dess kah)

complete (accomplish) – *kansei suru* (kahn-say sue-rue); *taisei* (tie-say)

Has the construction phase been completed?
> *Kenchiku wa kansei shimashita ka?*
> (ken-cheek-kuu wah kahn-say she-mahsh-tah kah)

compliment – *ohome* (oh-hoe-may)

Thank you for the compliment.
> *Ohome ni azukatte kyōshuku desu.*
> (oh-hoe-may nee ah-zuu-kah-tay k'yoe-shuu-kuu dess)

complimentary copy – *zōtei bon* (zoe-tay bone)

component – *kōsei yōso* (koe-say yoe-so); *konpo* (cone-poe)

composite materials – *fukugō zairyō* (fuu-kuu-go zye-rio)

compound interest – *fukuri* (fuu-kuu-ree)

compound semiconductor – *kagōbutsu handōtai* (kah-go-boot-sue hahn-doe-tie)

compromise – *enryō shiau* (en-rio she-ow); *dakyō suru* (dah-k'yoe sue-rue)

Unfortunately, there is no room for compromise.
Ainiku, dakyō no yochi ga arimasen. (eye-nee-kuu, dah-k'yoe no yoe-chee gah ah-ree-mah-sen)

comptroller – *kaikei kansa-yaku* (kye-kay kahn-sah-yah-kuu)

computer – *konpyūtā* (comb-pew-tah)

computer bank – *konpyūtā banku* (comb-pew-tah bahn-kuu)

computer center – *konpyūtā sentā* (comb-pew-tah sen-tah)

computer input – *konpyūtā nyūryoku* (comb-pew-tah n'yuu-rio-kuu)

computerized numerical control – *konpyūtā naizō sūchi seigyo sōchi* (comb-pew-tah nigh-zoe suu-chee say-g'yoe so-chee)

computer language – *konpyūtā gengo* (comb-pew-tah gen-go)

computer memory – *konpyūtā memorii* (comb-pew-tah may-moe-ree)

computer output – *konpyūtā shutsuryoku* (comb-pew-tah shoot-sue-rio-kuu)

computer program – *kompūtā puroguramu* (comb-pew-tah puu-roe-guu-rah-muu)

computer storage –*konpyūtā sutorēji* (comb-pew-tah stow-ray-jee)

computer terminal – *konpyūtā tāminaru* (comb-pew-tah tah-me-nah-rue)

conclude – *ketsuron wo dasu* (kate-sue-roan oh dah-sue)

I will give you a conclusion tomorrow.

Ashita ketsuron wo dashimasu.
(ah-shtah kate-sue-roan oh dah-she-mahss)

conclusion (concluding remarks) – *ketsuron* (kate-sue-roan); *teiketsu* (tay-kate-sue); final results – *ketsumatsu* (kate-sue-mah-t'sue)

The final results will be announced tomorrow afternoon.

Ketsuron wa ashita no gogo ni happyō shimasu.
(kate-sue-roan wah ah-shtah no go-go nee hop-p'yoe she-mahss)

condition (aspect) – *jōtai* (joe-tie)

What is the condition of that car?

Sono jidōsha no jōtai wa dō desu ka?
(so-no jee-doe-shah no joe-tie wah doe dess kah)

conditional acceptance – *jōken-tsuki hikiuke* (joe-ken-ski he-kee-uu-kay)

conditional sales contract – *jōken-tsuki baibai keiyaku* (joe-ken-ski by-by kay-yah-kuu)

conditions (terms) – *jōken* (joe-ken)

I will do it on condition that you help me.

Anata ga watakushi wo tetsudau jōken de sore wo hikiukemasu.
(ah-nah-tah gah wah-tock-she oh tay-t'sue-dow joe-ken day so-ray oh he-kee-uu-kay-mahss)

conference – *kaidan* (kye-dahn); *kaigi* (kye-ghee); *hanashi-ai* (hah-nah-she-eye)

What time will the conference begin?

Kaigi wa nanji ni hajimarimasu ka?
(kye-ghee wah nahn-jee nee hah-jee-mah-ree-mahss kah)

conference room – *kaigi shitsu* (kye-ghee sheet-sue)

confidential – *kimitsu no* (kee-meet-sue no)

confirm – *kakunin suru* (kah-kuu-neen sue-rue); *tashikameru* (tah-she-kah-may-rue)

Please confirm my airline reservations.

Watakushi no hikōki no yoyaku wo kakunin shite kudasai.

(wah-tock-she no he-koe-kee no yoe-yah-kuu oh kah-kuu-neen shtay kuu-dah-sigh)

confirmation of order – *chūmon kakunin* (chew-moan kah-kuu-neen)

confirmation slip; receipt – *kakunin sho* (kah-kuu-neen show)

confiscate – *bosshū suru* (boe-shuu sue-rue)

conflict of interest – *rigai no shōtotsu* (ree-guy-no show-tote-sue)

confrontation – *tairitsu* (tie-ree-t'sue)

Let us avoid a confrontation.

Tairitsu wo sakemashō.

(tie-ree-t'sue oh sah-kay-mah-show)

conglomerate – *fukugō kigyō* (fuu-kuu-go kee-g'yoe)

connecting flight – *noritsugi bin* (no-ree-t'sue-ghee bean)

What time does your connecting flight leave?

Anata no noritsugi bin wa nanji ni demasu ka?

(ah-nah-tah no no-ree-t'sue-ghee bean wah nahn-jee nee day-mahss kah)

consent (accept, agree) – *shōchi suru* (show-chee sue-rue)

I consent (accept).

Shōchi shimasu.

(show-chee she-mahss)

conservative (in color, style) – *jimi* (jee-me)

I want a suit that is very conservative.

Hijō ni jimi na sūtsu ga hoshii desu.

(he-joe nee jee-me nah suit-sue gah hoe-she dess)

consider – *kangaeru* (kahn-guy-rue)

I will give your proposal serious consideration.

Anata no mōshikomi wo shinken ni kangaete mimasu.

(ah-nah-tah no moe-she-koe-me oh sheen-ken kahn-guy-tay me-mahss)

consignee – *jutaku sha* (juu-tah-kuu shah)

consignment note – *itaku kamotsu unsō-jō* (ee-tah-kuu kah-moat-sue uun-so-joe)

consignment sales – *itaku hanbai* (ee-tah-kuu hahn-by); goods on consignment – *itaku hin* (ee-tah-kuu heen)

consolidated financial statement – *renketsu zaimu shohyō* (ren-kate-sue zye-muu show-h'yoe)

consolidated shipment – *renketsu shukka* (ren-kate-sue shuuk-kah)

consortium – *shakkan-dan* (shock-kahn-dahn)

construction – *kenchiku* (ken-chee-kuu); *kōji* (koe-jee)
Construction will start on the new building in January next year.
Atarashii biru no kenchiku wa rainen no ichigatsu kara hajimarimasu.
(ah-tah-rah-she bee-rue no ken-chee-kuu wah rye-nen no ee-chee-got-sue kah-rah hah-jee-mah-ree-mahss)

consular invoice – *ryōji shōmei okurijō* (rio-jee show-may oh-kuu-ree-joe)

consult (with you) – *sōdan suru* (so-dahn sue-rue)
I would like to consult with Mr. Kawahara about this matter.
Kono mondai wo Kawahara-san ni sōdan shitai desu.
(koe-no moan-dye oh kah-wah-hah-rah-sahn nee so-dahn she-tie dess)

consultant – *sōdanyaku* (so-dahn-yah-kuu)
He is a consultant for Mitsui Trading company.
Ano-hito wa Mitsui Bussan no sōdanyaku desu.
(ah-no-shtoe wa meet-sue-ee buse-sahn no so-dahn-yah-kuu dess)

consumer – *shōhisha* (show-he-shah); consumer goods
 – *shōhi zai* (show-he zye)

To be successful in Japan you must study the consumer market.

> *Nihon de seikō suru tame niwa shōhisha māketto
> wo benkyō shinakereba narimasen.*
>
> (nee-hone day say-koe sue-rue tah-may nee wah
> show-he-shah mah-kate-toe oh ben-k'yoe she-nah-
> kay-ray-bah nah-ree-mah-sen)

consumer acceptance – *shōhisha shōnin* (show-he-
shah show-neen)

consumer credit – *shōhisha shin'yō* (show-he-shah
sheen-yoe)

consumer goods – *shōhi zai* (show-he zye)

consumer price index – *shōhisha bukka shisū* (show-
he-shah buu-kah she-sue)

consumer research – *shōhisha chōsa* (show-he-shah
choe-sah)

consumer satisfaction – *shōhisha manzoku* (show-
he-shah mahn-zoe-kuu)

contact (get in touch with) – *renraku suru* (ren-rah-
kuu sue-rue)

Please get in touch with me next month.

> *Raigetsu renraku shite kudasai.*
>
> (rye-gate-sue ren-rah-kuu shtay kuu-dah-sigh)

May I contact you next week?

> *Raishū renraku shite mo ii desu ka?*
>
> (rye-shuu ren-rah-kuu shtay moe ee dess kah)

contact (someone you know) – *kone* (koe-nay);
sesshoku (say-show-kuu); personal contact – *kojin
sesshoku* (koe-jeen say-show-kuu)

I have no contacts in that company.

> *Watashi wa sono kaisha ni kone ga nai no desu.*
>
> (wah-tah-she wah so-no kye-shah nee cone-nay gah
> nigh no dess)

container – *kontena* (cone-tay-nah)

content (of medical preparation) – *yōryō* (yoe-rio)

contents (of box, etc.) – *naiyō* (nigh-yoe)
What is the contents of this box?
> *Kono hako no naiyō wa nan desu ka?*
> (koe-no hah-koe no nigh-yoe wah nahn dess kah)

contingencies – *fusoku jitai* (fuu-so-kuu jee-tie)

contingency fund – *kinkyū-yō tsumitate kin* (keen-cue-yoe t'sue-me-tah-tay keen)

contingent liability – *gūhatsu saimu* (guu-hot-sue sigh-muu)

contract – *keiyaku* (kay-yah-kuu); long-term contract – *chōki keiyaku* (choe-kee kay-yah-kuu)
The contract expires on April 1 next year.
> *Keiyaku wa rainen no shigatsu tsuitachi ni kiremasu.*
> (kay-yah-kuu wah rye-nen no she-got-sue t'sue-ee-tah-chee nee kee-ray-mahss)

contract carrier – *ukeoi unsō gyōsha* (uu-kay-oh-ee uun-so g'yoe-shah)

contract month – *keiyaku zuki* (kay-yah-kuu zuu-kee)

control by management – *shihai suru* (she-high sue-rue)

control by rules – *tōsei suru* (toe-say sue-rue)

controllable costs – *kanri-kanō hi* (kahn-ree-kah-no he)

controller – *kaikei kansayaku* (kye-kay kahn-sah-yah-kuu)

controlling interest – *shihai kenryoku* (she-high ken-rio-kuu)

converter (electrical) – *henkanki* (hen-kahn-kee)

convertible currency – *kōkan kanō tsūka* (koe-kahn kah-no t'sue-kah)

convertible debentures – *tenkan shasai* (ten-khan shah-sigh)

convertible preferred stock – *tenkan yūsen kabu* (ten-kahn yuu-sen kah-buu)

cooperation (collaboration) – *kyōryoku* (k'yoe-rio-kuu)
  I would like to ask you for your cooperation.
  Anata no go-kyōryoku wo yoroshiku onegai shimasu.
  (ah-nah-tah no go-k'yoe-rio-kuu oh yoe-roe-she-kuu oh-nay-guy she-mahss)

cooperative – *kyōdō kumiai* (k'yoe-doe kuu-me-eye)

cooperative advertising – *kyōdō kōkoku* (k'yoe-doe koe-koe-kuu)

co-ownership – *kyōdō shoyūken* (k'yoe-doe show-yuu-ken)

copy – *kopii* (koe-pee)
  Please make me ten copies of this report.
  Kono ripōto no kopii wo jūmai totte kudasai.
  (koe-no ree-poe-toe no koe-pee oh juu-my toe-tay kuu-dah-sigh)

copy (for advertising) – *kōkoku bun-an* (koe-koe-kuu boon-ahn)

copy (editorial manuscript) – *genkō* (gen-koe)

copy testing – *genkō chōsa* (gen-koe choe-sah)

copyright – *hanken* (hahn-ken); copyright reserved – *hanken shoyū* (hahn-ken show-yuu); *chosaku ken* (choe-sah-kuu ken)

cordless phone – *kōdoresu hon* (koe-doe-ray-sue hone)

corporate growth – *kigyō seichō* (kee-g'yoe say-choe)

corporate image – *kigyō imēji* (kee-g'yoe ee-may-jee)

corporate income tax – *hōjin zei* (hoe-jeen zay)

corporate planning – *kigyō keikaku* (kee-g'yoe kay-kah-kuu)

corporate structure – *jigyō keitai* (jee-g'yoe kay-tie)

corporate tax – *hōjin zei* (hoe-jeen zay)

corporation – *shadan hōjin* (shah-dahn hoe-jeen)
  Is your company incorporated?

Anata no kaisha wa shadan hōjin soshiki desu ka?
(ah-nah-tah no kye-shah wah sha-dan hoe-jeen so-she-kee dess kah)

corporation tax law – *hōjin zei hō* (hoe-jeen zay hoe)

correspondence – *tsūshin* (t'sue-sheen); *buntsū* (boon-t'sue)

correspondent bank – *torihiki-saki ginkō* (toe-ree-he-kee-sah-kee gheen-koe)

cost – *genka* (gen-kah)

cost (expense) – *hiyō* (he-yoe); *kosuto* (cost-oh)

cost accounting – *genka keisan* (gen-kah kay-sahn)

cost analysis – *genka bunseki* (gen-kah boon-say-kee)

cost and freight – *unchin komi nedan* (uun-cheen koe-me nay-dahn)

cost-benefit analysis – *hiyō-ben'eki bunseki* (he-yoe ben-ay-kee boon-say-kee)

cost control – *genka kanri* (gen-kah kahn-ree)

cost effectiveness – *genka nōritsu* (gen-kah no-ree-t'sue)

cost factor – *genka yōso* (gen-kah yoe-so)

cost of capital – *shihon kosuto* (she-hone cost-oh)

cost of goods sold – *uriage genka* (uu-ree-ah-gay gen-kah)

cost of living – *seikatsu hi* (say-cot-sue he)
The cost of living is still rising.
Seikatsu hi wa mada agatte imasu.
(say-cot-sue he wah mah-dah ah-got-tay ee-mahss)

cost of production – *genka* (gen-kah)

cost-plus – *genka kasan* (gen-kah kah-sahn)

cost-plus contract – *genka kasan keiyaku* (gen-kah kah-sahn kay-yah-kuu)

cost-price squeeze – *genka hikishime* (gen-kah he-kee-she-may)

cost reduction – *genka kirisage* (gen-kah kee-ree-sah-gay)

counter check – *yokin hikidashi hyō* (yoe-keen he-kee-dah-she h'yoe)

counterfeit – *gizō-hin* (ghee-zoe-heen)

countermeasure – *taisaku* (tie-sah-kuu); take countermeasures – *taisaku wo tateru* (tie-sah-kuu oh tah-tay-rue)

We must take a countermeasure.
Taisaku wo tatenakereba naranai desu.
(tie-sah-kuu oh tah-tay-nah-kay-ray-bah nah-rah-nigh dess)

country of origin – *gensan koku* (gen-sahn koe-kuu)

coupon (bond interest) – *rifuda* (ree-fuu-dah); *kūpon* (kuu-pone)

courier service – *takuhai bin* (tah-kuu-high bean)

courtesy visit – *aisatsu* (eye-sah-t'sue)

I have come to pay my respects to Mr. Sato.
Satō-san ni go-aisatsu ni ukagaimashita.
(sah-toe-sahn nee go-eye-sah-t'sue nee uu-kah-guy-mahsh-tah)

court of law – *hōtei* (hoe-tay); *saibansho* (sigh-bahn-show)

cover (of book or magazine) – *hyōshi* (h'yoe-she)

cover charge – *sābisu ryō* (sah-bee-sue rio); *oseki ryō* (oh-say-kee rio)

cover letter – *soe jō* (so-ay joe)

credit (financial) – *shin'yō* (sheen-yoe)

credit balance – *kashigata zandaka* (kah-she-gah-tah zahn-dah-kah)

credit bank – *shin'yō ginkō* (sheen-yoe gheen-koe)

credit bureau – *shōgyō kōshin-sho* (show-g'yoe koe-sheen-show)

credit card – *kurejitto kādo* (kuu-ray-jeet-toe kah-doe)

credit line – *shin'yō gendo-gaku* (sheen-yoe gen-doe-gah-kuu)

creditor – *saikensha* (sigh-ken-shah)

credit rating – *shin'yō kakuzuke* (sheen-yoe kah-kuu-zuu-kay)

credit reference – *shin'yō shōkai* (sheen-yoe show-kye)

credit terms – *shin'yō shiharai jōken* (sheen-yoe she-hah-rye joe-ken)

credit union – *shin'yō kumiai* (sheen-yoe kuu-me-eye)

criminal matter – *keiji mondai* (kay-jee moan-dye)

cross-licensing – *tokkyo ken kōkan* (toke-k'yoe ken koe-kahn)

cultivate; develop (a market) – *kaihatsu* (kye-hot-sue)
Developing a market is usually expensive.
> *Māketto wo kaihatsu suru no wa takai desu.*
> (mah-ket-toe oh kye-hot-sue sue-rue no wah tah-kye dess)

cumulative – *ruiseki-teki* (rue-ee-say-kee-tay-kee)

currency – *tsūka* (t'sue-kah)

currency band – *tsūka tai* (t'sue-kah tie)

currency clause – *tsūka yakkan* (t'sue-kah yah-kahn)

currency conversion – *tsūka kirikae* (t'sue-kah kee-ree-kye)

current account – *tōza kanjō* (toe-zah kahn-joe)

current assets – *ryūdō shisan* (r'yuu-doe she-sahn)

current checking account – *tōza yokin* (toe-zah yoe-keen)
Do you have a current checking account at Mitsubishi bank?
> *Mitsubishi ginkō ni tōza yokin ga arimasu ka?*
> (meet-sue-bee-she gheen-koe nee toe-zah yoe-keen gah ah-ree-mahss kah)

current liabilities – *ryūdō fusai* (r'yuu-doe fuu-sigh)

current ratio – *ryūdō hiritsu* (r'yuu-doe he-ree-t'sue)

current yield – *genzai rimawari* (gen-zye ree-mah-wah-ree)

customer – *kokyaku* (koe-k'yah-kuu)

customer service – *kokyaku sābisu* (koe-k'yah-kuu sah-bee-sue)

customs (behavior, practice) – *shūkan* (shuu-kahn)
It is important to know the customs of your business partners.
Bijinesu no aite no shūkan wo shitte iru no wa taisetsu na koto desu.
(bee-jee-nay-sue no eye-tay no shuu-kahn oh shtay ee-rue no wah tie-sate-sue nah koe-toe dess)

customs – *zeikan* (zay-kahn)

customs broker – *zeikan kamotsu toriatsukai nin* (zay-kahn kah-moat-sue toe-ree-ah-t'sue-kye neen)

customs duties – *kanzei* (kahn-zay)

customs entry – *zeikan tetsuzuki* (zay-kahn tate-sue-zuu-kee)

customs invoice – *zeikan okurijō* (zay-kahn oh-kuu-ree-joe)

cutback – *sakugen* (sah-kuu-gen)

cycle (long period of time) – *nagai toshitsuki* (nah-guy toe-sheet-sue-kee); cycle of events – *jiken no hanpuku* (jee-ken no hahn-puu-kuu); cycle of seasons – *kisetsu no utsurikawari* (key-sate-sue no uu-t'sue-ree-kah-wah-ree)

cycle billing – *seikyūsho no bunkatsu hakkō* (say-cue-show no boon-cot-sue hahk-koe)

— D —

daily – *mainichi* (my-nee-chee)
daily pay – *nikkyū* (neek-cue)
  I am paid by the day.
    Nikkyū de hataraite imasu.
    (neek-cue day hah-tah-rye-tay ee-mahss)
dairy products – *rakunō seihin* (rah-kuu-no say-heen)
damage; loss – *songai* (soan-guy)
  The rain caused a lot of damage.
    Ame ga daibu songai wo shimashita.
    (ah-may gah dye-buu soan-guy oh she-mahsh-tah)
dangerous – *abunai* (ah-buu-nigh); *kiken* (kee-ken);
  dangerous condition – *kiken na jōtai* (kee-ken nah
  joe-tie)
  Driving in Japanese cities is dangerous because of
  narrow streets.
    *Nihon no machi no semai michi de unten suru no
    wa kiken desu.*
    (nee-hone no mah-chee no say-my me-chee day
    uun-ten sue-rue no wah kee-ken dess)
data (information materials) – *shiryō* (she-rio)
  We do not yet have enough data to make a decision.
    Kettei suru ni wa mada shiryō ga tarinai.
    (kate-tay sue-rue nee wah mah-dah she-rio gah
    tah-ree-nigh)
data acquisition – *dētā shūshū* (day-tah shuu-shuu)
data bank – *dētā banku* (day-tah bahn-kuu)
data base – *dētā bēsu* (day-tah bay-sue)
date (of the month) – *hizuke* (he-zuu-kay)
  What is today's date?
    Kyō no hizuke wa nan desu ka?
    (k'yoe no he-zuu-kay wah nahn dess kah)

date of delivery – *ukewatashi bi* (uu-kay-wah-tah-she bee)

day – *hi* (he); *nichi* (nee-chee); what day – *nan nichi* (nahn nee-chee)

How many days will it take?
Nan nichi gurai kakarimasu ka?
(nahn nee-chee guu-rye kah-kah-ree-mahss kah)

dead freight – *kara-ni unchin* (kah-rah-nee uun-cheen)

deadline – *saishū kigen* (sigh-shuu kee-gen)

deadlock – *ikizumari* (ee-kee-zuu-mah-ree)

deal – *torihiki* (toe-ree-he-kee)

dealer – *diira* (dee-rah)

dealership – *hanbai-ken* (hahn-by-ken)

deal with – *torihiki suru* (toe-ree-he-kee sue-rue)

I do not want to deal with that company.
Sono kaisha to wa torihiki shitaku nai.
(so-no kye-shah toe wah toe-ree-he-kee she-tah-kuu nigh)

debentures – *shasai* (shah-sigh)

debit – *karigata* (kah-ree-gah-tah)

debt – *shakkin* (shock-keen); *fusai* (fuu-sigh)

That company is always in debt.
Sono kaisha wa itsumo shakkin shiteimasu.
(so-no kye-shah wah eat-sue-moe shahk-keen shtay-mahss)

debug (computer program) – *debaggu suru* (day-bug-guu sue-rue)

decision – *kettei* (kate-tay); prompt decision – *sokudan* (so-kuu-dahn)

When will you make a decision?
Kettei wa itsu shimasu ka?
(kate-tay wah eat-sue she-mahss kah)

decline (decay) – *suitai suru* (sue-ee-tie sue-rue)

That industry is now declining.

Sono kōgyō wa ima suitai shiteimasu.
(so-no koe-g'yoe wah ee-mah sue-ee-tye shtay-mahss)

decrease – *herasu* (hay-rah-sue)
  Our profits have been decreasing since last year.
  Kaisha no rieki wa kyonen kara hette imasu.
  (kye-shah no ree-ay-kee wah k'yoe-nen kah-rah hate-tay ee-mahss)

deductible – *kōjo dekiru* (koe-joe day-kee-rue)

deduction – *kōjo* (koe-joe)

deed – *shōsho* (show-show)

deed of sale – *uriwatashi shōsho* (uu-ree-wah-tah-she show-show)

deed of transfer – *meigi kakikae shōsho* (may-ghee kah-kee-kye show-show)

deed of trust – *shintaku shōsho* (sheen-tah-kuu show-show)

default – *saimu rikō wo okotaru* (sigh-muu ree-koe oh oh-koe-tah-rue)

defect – *kekkan* (cake-kahn); defective product – *kekkan shōhin* (cake-kahn show-heen)

defective – *kekkan ga aru* (cake-kahn gah ah-rue)

deferred annuities – *sueoki nenkin* (sway-oh-kee nen-keen)

deferred assets – *kurinobe shisan* (kuu-ree-no-bay she-sahn)

deferred charges – *kurinobe hiyō* (kuu-ree-no-bay he-yoe)

deferred delivery – *nobe watashi* (no-bay wah-tah-she)

deferred income – *kurinobe shūeki* (kuu-ree-no-bay shuu-ay-kee)

deferred liabilities – *sueoki fusai* (sway-oh-kee fuu-sigh)

deferred tax – *sueoki zei* (sway-oh-kee zay)

deficit – *akaji* (ah-kah-jee)
  We suffered a deficit all last year.
    Kyōnen-jū akaji deshita.
    (k'yoe-nen-juu ah-kah-jee desh-tah)
deficit financing – *akaji zaisei* (ah-kah-jee zye-say)
deficit spending – *chōka shishutsu* (choe-kah she-shoot-sue)
deflation – *tsūka shūshuku* (t'sue-kah shuu-shuu-kuu)
degree (grade) – *teido* (tay-doe)
  I agree with you to some degree.
    Aru teido made wa sansei shite imasu.
    (ah-rue tay-doe mah-day wah sahn-say shtay ee-mahss)
delay – *entai* (en-tie)
delinquent account – *shiharai entai kanjō* (she-hah-rye en-tie kahn-joe)
deliver (small things) – *todokeru* (toe-doe-kay-rue)
  Please deliver this package to Mr. Taro Fujimoto.
    Kono nimotsu wo Fujimoto Tarō-san ni todokete kudasai.
    (koe-no nee-moat-sue oh fuu-jee-moe-toe tah-roe-sahn nee toe-doe-kay-tay kuu-dah-sigh)
delivered price – *hikiwatashi nedan* (he-kee-wah-tah-she nay-dahn)
deliver goods – *nōhin suru* (no-heen sue-rue); statement of delivery – *nōhin sho* (no-heen show)
  Please deliver (these goods) to the warehouse.
    Sōko e nōhin shite kudasai.
    (so-koe ay no-heen shtay kuu-dah-sigh)
delivery – *hikiwatashi* (he-kee-wah-tah-she)
delivery date – *nōki* (no-kee)
delivery notice – *hikiwatashi tsūchi-sho* (he-kee-wah-tah-she t'sue-chee-show)
delivery points – *ukewatashi basho* (uu-kay-wah-tah-she bah-show)

delivery price (shipping) – *unchin komi nedan* (uun-cheen koe-me nay-dahn)

delivery price (securities) – *ukewatashi hyōjun nedan* (uu-kay-wah-tah-she h'yoe-june nay-dahn)

demand deposit – *yōkyū barai yokin* (yoe-cue bah-rye yoe-keen)

demographic – *jinkō tōkei gaku-jō no* (jeen-koe toe-kay gah-kuu-joe no)

demotion – *kakusage* (kah-kuu-sah-gay)

department – *bumon* (buu-moan)

department manager (in a company) – *buchō* (buu-choe)

department store – *depāto* (day-pah-toe)

departure gate – *tōjō guchi* (toe-joe guu-chee)
Let's meet at the departure gate.
Tōjō guchi de aimashō.
(toe-joe guu-chee day eye-mah-show)

deposit (bank account) – *ginkō yokin* (gheen-koe yoe-keen); leave something with someone (individual or baggage claim, etc.) – *azukeru* (ah-zuu-kay-rue)

deposit for security purposes – *hoshō kin* (hoe-show keen)

deposit in advance – *atama kin* (ah-tah-mah keen)

deposit when renting a house or apartment (returnable) – *shikikin* (she-kee-keen)

deposit when renting a house or apartment (not returnable) – *kenrikin* (ken-ree-keen)

depreciation – *kachi-geraku* (kah-chee-gay-rah-kuu)

depreciation allowance – *genka shōkyaku hikiate kin* (gen-kah show-k'yah-kuu he-kee-ah-tay keen)

depreciation of currency – *tsūka teiraku* (t'sue-kah tay-rah-kuu)

depression (economic) – *fukeiki* (fuu-kay-kee)

deputy (agent) – *dairi* (dye-ree)

deputy chairman – *fuku kaichō* (fuu-kuu kye-choe)

deputy manager – *fuku shihainin* (fuu-kuu she-high-neen)

design – *dezain* (day-zine)

design engineering – *dezain kōgaku* (day-zine koe-gah-kuu)

designer – *dezainā* (day-zye-nah)

desktop calculator – *dentaku* (den-tah-kuu)

destination – *ikisaki* (ee-kee-sah-kee); *yukisaki* (yuu-kee-sah-kee)

Where is your final destination?

Saigo no ikisaki wa doko desu ka?

(sigh-go no ee-kee-sah-kee wah doe-koe dess kah)

details – *shōsai* (show-sigh)

Please explain the details of the contract.

Keiyaku no shōsai wo setsumei shite kudasai.

(kay-yah-kuu no show-sigh oh say-t'sue-may shtay kuu-dah-sigh)

devaluation – *heika kirisage* (hay-kah kee-ree-sah-gay)

develop (photograph) – *genzō suru* (gen-zoe sue-rue)

develop (reclaim) – *kaitaku* (kye-tah-kuu)

The factory is on reclaimed land.

Kōjō wa kaitaku sareta tochi ni arimasu.

(koe-joe wah kye-tah-kuu sah-ray-tah toe-chee nee ah-ree-mahss)

developing country – *kōshin koku* (koe-sheen koe-kuu)

development; growth – *kaihatsu* (kye-hot-sue); gradual progress – *hatten suru* (hot-ten sue-rue); expansion – *kakuchō* (kah-kuu-choe); development expense – *kaihatsu hi* (kye-hot-sue he)

diesel (engine) – *diizeru* (dee-zay-rue)

digital – *dejitaru* (day-jee-tah-rue)

digital audio disc – *dejitaru ōdio disuku* (day-jee-tah-rue oh-dee-oh disk-uu)

digital audio tape recorder – *dejitaru ōdio tēpu rekōda* (day-jee-tah-rue oh-dee-oh tay-puu ray-koe-dah)

dilution of equity – *mochi-kabu hiritsu no teika* (moe-chee-kah-buu he-ree-t'sue no tay-kah)

direct access storage – *chokusetsu akusesu sutorēji* (choke-say-t'sue ah-kuu-say-sue stow-ray-jee)

direct cost – *chokusetsu hi* (choke-say-t'sue he)

direct expense – *chokusetsu keihi* (choke-say-t'sue kay-he)

direct investment – *chokusetsu tōshi* (choke-say-t'sue toe-she)

direct line – *choku tsū* (choke t'sue)
When you call, use the direct line.
> *Denwa wo kakeru toki niwa choku tsū wo tsukatte kudasai.*
> (den-wah oh kah-kay-rue toe-kee nee-wah choke t'suu oh scot-tay kuu-dah-sigh)

direct mail – *dairekuto mēru* (dye-reck-toe may-rue)

director of a company – *torishimariyaku* (toe-ree-she-mah-ree-yah-kuu); chairman of the board – *riji chō* (ree-jee choe).

direct quotation – *chokusetsu sōba* (choke-say-t'sue so-bah)

direct sales shop/store – *choku bai ten* (choke by ten)

direct selling – *chokusetsu hanbai* (choke-say-t'sue hahn-by)

direct tax – *chokusetsu zei* (choke-say-t'sue zay)

disbursement – *shiharai* (she-hah-rye)

discharge (fire) – *kaiko suru* (kye-koe sue-rue)

discount – *waribiki* (wah-ree-bee-kee); *waribiki ritsu* (wah-ree-bee-kee ree-t'sue)
If I pay in cash how much discount will you give me?
> *Genkin de haraeba ikura ka waribiki shite itadakemasu ka?*

  (gen-keen day hah-rah-ay-bah ee-kuu-rah kah wah-
  ree-bee-kee shtay ee-tah-dah-kee-mahss kah)

discount rate – *tegata waribiki buai* (tay-gah-tah
  wah-ree-bee-kee buu-eye)

discretionary income – *nakagai inin shotoku* (nah-
  kah-guy ee-neen show-toe-kuu)

discretionary order – *nakagai inin chūmon* (nah-
  kah-guy ee-neen chew-moan)

disk – *disuku* (disk-uu)

dismiss; let go – *ikaseru* (ee-kah-say-rue); *kaiko* (kye-
  koe)

  Business is slow so I let him go.
    *Bijinesu ga fuchō desu node kare wo kaiko
    shimashita.*
    (bee-jee-ness gah fuu-choe dess no-day kah-ray oh
    kye-koe she-mahsh-tah)

dispatch, send (shipment, goods) – *shukka suru*
  (shuuk-kah sue-rue)

display unit – *disupurei sōchi* (dis-puu-ray so-chee)

disposable income – *shobun-kanō shotoku* (show-
  boon-kah-no show-toe-kuu)

dispute – *sōgi* (so-ghee); to dispute something – *ronsō
  suru* (roan-so sue-rue)

distribution – *ryūtsū* (r'yuu-t'sue)

distribution channel – *ryūtsū keiro* (r'yuu-t'sue kay-
  roe); *ryūtsū channeru* (r'yuu-t'sue chah-nay-rue)

distribution costs – *ryūtsū kosuto* (r'yuu-t'sue cost-oh)

distribution network – *ryūtsū mō* (r'yuu-t'sue moe)

distribution policy (securities) – *bunpai hō* (boom-
  pie hoe)

distribution policy (goods) – *ryūtsū seisaku* (r'yuu-
  t'sue say-sah-kuu)

distributor (of goods) – *motouri sabaki nin* (moe-toe-
  uu-ree sah-bah-kee neen)

diversification (business) – *takaku keiei-ka* (tah-kah-kuu kay-ay-kah)

divestment – *kenri sōshitsu* (ken-ree so-sheet-sue)

dividend – *haitō* (high-toe)
  That company pays a large dividend every year.
    Sono kaisha wa mainen ōkii haitō wo haraimasu.
    (so-no kye-shah wah my-nen oh-kee high-toe oh hah-rye-mahss)

dividend yield – *haitō rimawari* (high-toe ree-mah-wah-ree)

division of labor – *bungyō* (boon-g'yoe)

do business with – *torihiki suru* (toe-ree-he-kee sue-rue)

dock handling charges – *senkyo kamotsu toriatsukai hi* (sen-k'yoe kah-moat-sue toe-ree-ah-t'sue-kye he)

dock receipt – *dokku uketori-shō* (doke-kuu uu-kay-toe-ree-show)

doctorate, Ph.D. – *hakase* (hah-kah-say); Doctor Ito – *Ito Hakase* (ee-toe hah-kah-say)

documents (official papers) – *shorui* (show-rue-ee)
  Are these all of the documents that are needed?
    Kore wa hitsuyō na shorui no zenbu desu ka?
    (koe-ray wah heat-sue-yoe nah show-rue-ee no zem-buu dess kah)

dollar cost averaging – *doru heikin hō* (doe-rue hay-keen hoe)

domestic – *kokunai* (koe-kuu-nigh)
  This product is not sold in the domestic market.
    Kono shinamono wa kokunai no māketto de wa urareteimasen.
    (koe-no she-nah-moe-no wah koe-kuu-nigh no mah-ket-toe day wah uu-rah-ray-tay-mah-sen)

domestic bill – *kokunai tegata* (koe-kuu-nigh tay-gah-tah)

domestic company – *kokunai gaisha* (coke-nigh guy-shah)

door-to-door sales – *kobetsu hōmon hanbai* (koe-bay-t'sue hoe-moan hahn-by)

double-entry bookkeeping – *fuku-shiki boki* (fuu-kuu-she-kee boe-kee)

double pricing – *nijū kakaku* (nee-juu kah-kah-kuu)

double taxation – *nijū kazei* (nee-juu kah-zay)

double time – *chingin baigaku-barai* (cheen-gheen by-gah-kuu-bah-rye)

downpayment – *atama kin* (ah-tah-mah keen)

down period – *kōjō heisa kikan* (koe-joe hay-sah kee-khan)

down-time – *sagyō-ichiji chūshi-jikan* (sah-g'yoe-ee-chee-jee chew-she-jee-kahn)

down-turn – *chintai* (cheen-tie)

draft (bank) – *tegata furidashi* (tay-gah-tah fuu-ree-dah-she)

draft (of document) – *shita-gaki* (she-tah-gah-kee)

drawback (money) – *modoshi zei* (moe-doe-she zay)

draw down – *hiki orosu* (he-kee oh-roe-sue)

drawee (of draft) – *tegata na-ate nin* (tay-gah-tah nah-ah-tay neen)

drawer (of draft) – *tegata furidashi nin* (tay-gah-tah fuu-ree-dah-she neen)

drop-shipment – *seisan-sha chokusō* (say-sahn-shah choke-so)

dry cargo – *kan ni* (kahn nee)

dry goods (grain) – *koku rui* (koe-kuu rue-ee)

dry goods (textiles) – *ori mono* (oh-ree moe-no)

dummy (mockup of a printing project) – *teisai mihon* (tay-sigh me-hone)

dumping – *danpingu* (dahm-peen-guu)

dun (for payment) – *kibishiku saisoku suru* (kee-bee-she-kuu sigh-so-kuu sue-rue)

durable – *jōbu na* (joe-buu nah)
  If these are not durable I don't want them.
    Kore wa jōbu janakattara irimasen.
    (koe-ray wah joe-buu jah-nah-kah-tah-rah ee-ree-
    mah-sen)
durable goods – *taikyū zai* (tie-cue zye)
duty (honor bound, obligation) – *gimu* (ghee-muu)
  It is my duty to work as hard as I can.
    *Dekiru dake shigoto wo suru no ga watakushi no
    gimu desu.*
    (day-kee-rue dah-kay she-go-toe oh sue-rue no gah
    wah-tock-she no ghee-muu dess)
duty (customs fees) – *kanzei* (kahn-zay)
duty-free – *menzei no* (men-zay no)
duty-free goods – *menzei hin* (men-zay heen)

— E —

earnest money – *tetsuke kin* (tay-t'sue-kay keen)

earnings (profit) – *rieki* (ree-ay-kee)

We will not make a profit this year.

Kotoshi wa rieki ga demasen.

(koe-toe-she wah ree-ay-kee gah day-mah-sen)

earnings on assets – *shisan shotoku* (she-sahn show-toe-kuu)

earnings per share – *hito-kabu atari no rieki* (he-toe-kah-buu ah-tah-ree no ree-ay-kee)

earnings/price ratio – *shūeki kabu-ka ritsu* (shuu-ay-kee kah-buu-kah ree-t'sue)

earnings report – *shūeki hōkoku* (shuu-ay-kee hoe-koe-kuu)

earnings retained – *horyū rieki* (hoe-r'yuu ree-ay-kee)

economic – *keizai no* (kay-zye no)

economical – *keizai-teki* (kay-zye-tay-kee)

economic barometer – *keizai kansoku shisū* (kay-zye kahn-so-kuu she-sue)

economic indicators – *keizai shihyō* (kay-zye she-h'yoe)

According to economic indicators this year looks good.

Keizai shihyō ni yoru to kotoshi wa yosasō desu.

(kay-zye she-h'yoe nee yoe-rue toe koe-toe-she wa yoe-sah-so dess)

economic mission – *keizai shisetsu* (kay-zye she-say-t'sue)

economic prospects – *keizai mitōshi* (kay-zye me-toe-she)

What are the economic prospects for that country?

Sono kuni no keizai mitōshi wa dō nan desu ka?

(so-no kuu-nee no kay-zye me-toe-she wah doe
nahn dess kah)

economics – *keizai gaku* (kay-zye gah-kuu)

economic trend – *keizai dōkō* (kay-zye doe-koe)
There is some concern about future economic trends.
Kongo no keizai dōkō ga ki ni narimasu.
(cone-go no kay-zye doe-koe gah kee nee nah-ree-
mahss)

economize – *setsuyaku suru* (say-t'sue-yah-kuu sue-
rue)

economy – *keizai* (kay-zye)

economy of scale – *kibo no keizai* (kee-boe no kay-zye)

edit (writing) – *henshū suru* (hen-shuu sue-rue)

editor – *henshū-sha* (hen-shuu-shah)

educate; train – *kyōiku suru* (k'yoe-ee-kuu sue-rue)
Employee training is very important.
Shain kyōiku wa totemo taisetsu na koto desu.
(shah-een k'yoe-ee-kuu wah toe-tay-moe tie-say-
t'sue nah koe-toe dess)

efficiency – *kōritsu* (koe-ree-t'sue); improvement in efficiency – *kōritsu-ka suru* (koe-ree-t'sue-kah sue-rue)

effort (exertion, attempt) – *doryoku* (doe-rio-kuu)

effort, make an – *chikara wo tsukusu* (chee-kah-rah
oh t'sue-kuu-sue)
I will extend my best effort.
Dekiru dake chikara wo tsukushimasu.
(day-kee-rue dah-kay chee-kah-rah oh t'sue-kuu-
she-mahss)

eight-hour-a-day system – *hachi-ji-kan sei* (hah-chee-
jee-kahn say)

elasticity (supply/demand) – *danryoku sei* (dahn-rio-
kuu say)

elections – *senkyo* (sen-k'yoe)

electric – *denki no* (den-kee no)

electrical engineering – *denki kōgaku* (den-kee koe-
gah-kuu)

electrical product – *denki seihin* (den-kee say-heen)

electrical resistance – *denki teikō* (den-kee tay-koe)

electrically conductive – *dendō sei* (den-doe say)

electric heater – *denki danbōki* (den-kee dahn-boe-
kee)

electric circuit – *denki kairo* (den-kee kye-roe)

electric shaver – *denki higesori* (den-kee he-gay-so-
ree)

electric tools – *denki kōgu* (den-kee koe-guu)

electricity – *denki* (den-kee)

electronic desk calculator – *takujō denshi keisanki*
(tah-kuu-joe den-she kay-sahn-kee)

electronics – *denshi kōgaku* (den-she koe-gah-kuu)

electronic typewriter – *denshi taipuraita* (den-she
type-rye-tah)

embargo – *tsūshō teishi* (t'sue-show tay-she)

embezzlement – *ōryō* (oh-rio)

emergency – *hijōji* (he-joe-jee)
Emergency!
Hijōji desu!
(he-joe-jee dess)

emergency measures – *kyūsaku* (cue-sah-kuu)

emotional – *jōjō-teki* (joe-joe-tay-kee)
Japanese businessmen are often very emotional.
*Nihon-jin no bijinesuman wa tama ni sugoku jōjō-
teki desu.*
(nee-hone-jeen no bee-jee-nay-sue-mahn wah tah-
mah nee joe-joe-tay-kee dess)

employee – *jūgyō-in* (juu-g'yoe-een); office employee –
jimu-in (jee-muu-een)

employee counseling – *jūgyō-in sōdan-seido* (juu-
g'yoe-een so-dahn-say-doe)

employee relations – *jūgyō-in kankei* (juu-g'yoe-een kahn-kay)

employment – *koyō* (koe-yoe); employment terms – *koyō jōken* (koe-yoe joe-ken)

employment agency – *shokugyō shōkai-jo* (show-kuu-g'yoe show-kye-joe)

encounter; oppose – *taisen* (tie-sen)

end of period – *kimatsu* (kee-mot-sue)

endorse – *uragaki suru* (uu-rah-gah-kee sue-rue)
    Please endorse this check.
        Kono kogitte ni uragaki shite kudasai.
        (koe-no koe-gheet-tay nee uu-rah-gah-kee shtay kuu-dah-sigh)

endorsee – *hi-uragaki-nin* (he-uu-rah-gah-kee-neen)

endorsement – *uragaki* (uu-rah-gah-kee)

endorser – *uragaki-nin* (uu-rah-gah-kee-neen)

endowment – *zaisan kizō* (zye-sahn kee-zoe)

end product – *saishū seisan-butsu* (sigh-shuu say-sahn-boot-sue)

end-use certificate – *saishū yōto shōmeisho* (sigh-shuu yoe-toe show-may-show)

engineer – *gishi* (ghee-she)

engineering – *kōgaku* (koe-gah-kuu)

engineering design department – *gijutsu sekkei bumon* (ghee-jute-sue sake-kay buu-moan)

engrave (for printing) – *horu* (hoe-rue)

enlarge – *kakudai suru* (kah-kuu-dye sue-rue)
    Can you enlarge this?
        Kore wo kakudai suru koto ga dekimasu ka?
        (koe-ray oh kah-kuu-dye sue-rue koe-toe gah day-kee-mahss kah)

enlarge (a photograph) – *hikinobasu* (he-kee-no-bah-sue)

enlarger – *hikinobashi-ki* (he-kee-no-bah-she-kee)

enterprise – *kigyō* (kee-g'yoe); **enterprising** – *sekkyoku-teki* (sake-yoe-kuu-tay-kee)

enterprise taxes – *jigyō zei* (jee-g'yoe zay)

enterprise union – *kigyō nai kumiai* (kee-g'yoe nigh kuu-me-eye)

entertainment – *yokyō* (yoe-k'yoe); *asobi* (ah-so-bee); *goraku* (go-rah-kuu)

entertainment expense – *kōsai hi* (koe-sigh he)
About how much entertainment expense do you use each month?
Mai tsuki dono gurai no kōsai hi wo tsukaemasu ka?
(my ski doe-no guu-rye no koe-sigh he oh sky-mahss kah)

entertainment trades – *kōgyō* (koe-g'yoe)

entrepreneur – *kigyō-ka* (kee-g'yoe-kah); *anto-purenua* (ahn-toe-puu-ray-nuu-ah)

entry permit – *tsūkan menkyo* (t'sue-kahn men-k'yoe)

entry visa – *nyūgoku sashō* (new-go-kuu sah-show)

environment – *kankyō* (kahn-k'yoe)

equal – *dōitsu* (doe-eat-sue)

equalize – *kintō ni suru* (keen-toe nee sue-rue)

equal pay for equal work – *dōitsu rōdō dōitsu chingin* (doe-eat-sue roe-doe doe-eat-sue cheen-gheen)

equipment – *setsubi* (say-t'sue-bee)
Is all of this equipment new?
Kono setsubi wa zenbu atarashii desu ka?
(koe-no say-t'sue-bee wah zem-buu ah-tah-rah-she dess kah)

equity – *mochibun* (moe-chee-boon)
How much equity does he have in that company?
Sono kaisha ni ano hito wa dono gurai no mochibun wo motte imasu ka?
(so-no kye-shah nee ah-no shtoe wah doe-no guu-rye no moe-chee-boon oh moat-tay ee-mahss kah)

equity investments – *chokusetsu shusshi* (choke-say-t'sue shuu-she)

error – *erā* (ay-rah)

Please be careful not to make any errors.

Erā wo shinai yō ni ki wo tsukete kudasai.

(ay-rah oh she-nigh yoe nee kee oh skate-tay kuu-dah-sigh)

escalator clause – *esukarētā jōkō* (es-kah-ray-tah joe-koe)

escape clause – *menseki jōkō* (men-say-kee joe-koe)

Is there an escape clause in the contract?

Keiyaku ni menseki jōkō ga arimasu ka?

(kay-yah-kuu nee men-say-kee joe-koe gah ah-ree-mahss kah)

escrow – *jōken tsuki jōto shōsho* (joe-ken ski joe-toe show-show)

escrow account – *esukurō akaunto* (ess-kuu-roe ah-count-oh)

establish – *setsuritsu suru* (say-t'sue-ree-t'sue sue-rue)

I/we will establish a new company.

Atarashii kaisha wo setsuritsu shimasu.

(ah-tah-rah-she kye-shah oh say-t'sue-ree-t'sue she-mahss)

estate – *shisan* (she-sahn)

estate agent – *zaisan kanri nin* (zye-sahn kahn-ree neen)

estate tax – *isan sōzoku zei* (ee-sahn so-zoe-kuu zay)

estimate – *mitsumori* (meet-sue-moe-ree); written estimate – *mitsumori sho* (meet-sue-moe-ree show); to estimate – *mitsumoru* (meet-sue-moe-rue)

estimate cost – *nebumi suru* (nay-buu-me sue-rue)

estimated price – *mitsumori kakaku* (meet-sue-moe-ree kah-kah-kuu)

Of course, that is just an estimated price.

Mochiron, sore wa mitsumori kakaku desu.

(moe-chee-roan so-ray wah meet-sue-moe-ree kah-kah-kuu dess)

estimated time of arrival – *tōchaku yotei jikoku* (toe-chah-kuu yoe-tay jee-koe-kuu)

When is Mr. Kawabata's estimated time of arrival?

Kawabata-san no tōchaku yotei jikoku wa nanji desu ka?

(kah-wah-bah-tah-sahn no toe-chah-kuu yoe-tay jee-koe-kuu wah nahn-jee dess kah)

estimated time of departure – *shuppatsu yotei jikoku* (shuup-pot-sue yoe-tay jee-koe-kuu)

ethics – *dōtoku* (doe-toe-kuu)

Eurobond – *Yūro bondo* (yuu-roe bone-doe)

Eurocurrency – *Yūro tsūka* (yuu-roe t'sue-kah)

Eurodollar – *Yūro darā* (yuu-roe dah-rah)

Europe – *Yoroppa* (yoe-roe-pah); Europe-oriented – *Yoroppa-muke* (yoe-roe-pah-muu-kay); European Community — *ii-shi* (ee-she)

evaluation – *hyōka* (h'yoe-kah)

examine; study; consider – *kentō suru* (ken-toe sue-rue)

I will study/consider your idea.

Anata no kangae wo kentō shimasu.

(ah-nah-tah no kahn-guy oh ken-toe she-mahss)

example (for) – *ichi rei* (ee-chee ray)

excess demand – *chōka juyō* (choe-kah juu-yoe)

excessive packaging – *kajō hōsō* (kah-joe hoe-so)

exchange (barter) – *kōkan* (koe-kahn)

Will barter be acceptable to you?

Kōkan shite itadakemasu ka?

(koe-kahn shtay ee-tah-dah-kee-mahss kah)

exchange (stocks, commodities) – *torihiki-sho* (toe-ree-he-kee-show)

exchange control – *gaikoku kawase kanri* (guy-koe-kuu kah-wah-say kahn-ree)

exchange discount – *kawase waribiki* (kah-wah-say wah-ree-bee-kee)

exchange loss – *kawase sason* (kah-wah-say sah-soan)

exchange market – *gaikoku kawase shijō* (guy-koe-kuu kah-wah-say she-joe)

exchange name cards – *meishi kōkan* (may-she koe-kahn)

exchange rate – *gaikoku kawase sōba* (guy-koe-kuu kah-wah-say so-bah)

What is today's exchange rate?

   Kyō no gaikoku kawase sōba wa nan desu ka? (k'yoe no guy-koe-kuu kah-wah-say so-bah wah nahn dess kah)

exchange risk – *kawase risuku* (kah-wah-say risk-uu)

exchange value – *kōkan kachi* (koe-kahn kah-chee)

excise duty – *shōhi zei* (show-he zay)

excise license – *menkyo zei* (men-k'yoe zay)

exclude – *nozoku* (noe-zoe-kuu); *nozoite* (no-zoe-ee-tay)

exclusive – *senzoku* (sen-zoe-kuu)

exclusive agency – *senzoku tokuyakuten* (sen-zoe-kuu toe-kuu-yah-kuu-ten)

exclusive agent – *itte dairi ten* (eat-tay dye-ree ten)

ex dividend – *haitō ochi* (high-toe oh-chee)

ex dock – *futō watashi* (fuu-toe wah-tah-she)

executive – *keiei kanbu* (kay-ay kahn-buu); *jūyaku* (juu-yah-kuu)

executive board – *jōnin riji kai* (joe-neen ree-jee kye)

executive committee – *jōmu shikkō i-inkai* (joe-muu sheek-koe ee-een-kye)

executive compensation – *kanbu yakuin hōshū* (kahn-buu yah-kuu-een hoe-shuu)

executive director – *senmu torishimariyaku* (sem-muu toe-ree-she-mah-ree-yah-kuu)

executive secretary – *jimu kyokuchō* (jee-muu k'yoe-kuu-choe)

executive session – *jikkō i-in kaigi* (jee-koe ee-een kye-ghee)

executive staff – *kanbu* (kahm-buu)

executor – *shitei yuigon shikkō sha* (she-tay yuu-ee-goan sheek-koe shah)

exempt from taxes – *men zei* (men zay)

exemption – *menjo* (men-joe)

ex factory – *kōjō watashi* (koe-joe wah-tah-she)

expand – *kasamu* (kah-sah-muu)

expectation; aspect – *yosō* (yoe-so)

expected results (profits) – *kitai rieki* (kee-tie ree-ay-kee)

expenditure(s) – *shishutsu* (she-shoot-sue)

expense account – *settai hi* (set-tie he)

expenses – *keihi* (kay-he)

expenses for eating and drinking – *inshoku hi* (een-show-kuu he)

expert (technical or scientific) – *senmonka* (sem-moan-kah); expert in doing things – *kuroto* (kuu-roe-toe)
He is a computer specialist.
Ano hito wa konpyūtā no senmonka desu.
(ah-no shtoe wah cone-pew-tah no sem-moan-kah dess)

explain – *setsumei suru* (say-t'sue-may sue-rue)
Please explain the last part again.
Mō ichido saigō no tokoro wo setsumei shite kudasai.
(moe ee-chee-doe sigh-go no toe-koe-roe oh say-t'sue-may shtay kuu-dah-sigh)

exploitation – *kaisetsu* (kye-say-t'sue)

export – *yushutsu suru* (yuu-shoot-sue sue-rue)

export agent – *yushutsu dairiten* (yuu-shoot-sue dye-ree-ten)

export ban – *yushutsu kinshi* (yuu-shoot-sue keen-she)

export broker – *yushutsu burōka* (yuu-shoot-sue buu-roe-kah)

export company – *yushutsu gyōsha* (yuu-shoot-sue g'yoe-shah)

export credit – *yushutsu shin'yō jō* (yuu-shoot-sue sheen-yoe joe)

export duty – *yushutsu kanzei* (yuu-shoot-sue kahn-zay)

export entry – *yushutsu shinkoku sho* (yuu-shoot-sue sheen-koe-kuu show)

export-import bank – *yushutsu-nyū ginkō* (yuu-shoot-sue-n'yuu gheen-koe)

export license – *yushutsu kyokasho* (yuu-shoot-sue k'yoe-kah-show)

Do you have an export license?
Yushutsu kyokasho wo motte imasu ka?
(yu-shoot-sue k'yoe-kah-show oh moat-tay ee-mahss kah)

export manager – *yushutsu kachō* (yuu-shoot-sue kah-choe)

export permit – *yushutsu kyoka* (yuu-shoot-sue k'yoe-kah)

export quota – *yushutsu wariate* (yuu-shoot-sue wah-ree-ah-tay)

There is no export quota on wooden products.
Moku seihin ni yushutsu wariate wa arimasen.
(moe-kuu say-heen nee yuu-shoot-sue wah-ree-ah-tay wah ah-ree-mah-sen)

export regulations – *yushutsu kisei* (yuu-shoot-sue kee-say)

export restrictions – *yushutsu seigen* (yuu-shoot-sue say-gen)

export sales contract – *yushutsu hanbai keiyaku* (yuu-shoot-sue hahn-by kay-yah-kuu)

export tax – *yushutsu-hin zei* (yuu-shoot-sue-heen zay)

exposure (photography) – *roshutsu* (roe-shoot-sue)

exposure meter – *roshutsu kei* (roe-shoot-sue kay)

expression (colloquialism) – *hyōgen* (h'yoe-gen)

express train – *kyūkō ressha* (cue-koe ray-shah)

expropriation – *chōshū* (choe-shuu)

ex rights – *kenri ochi* (ken-ree oh-chee)

ex ship – *chakusen watashi* (chock-sen wah-tah-she)

extend; extension – *enchō suru* (en-choe sue-rue);

extension of time – *jikan no enchō* (jee-kahn no en-choe)

I would like to get a one-year extension on the contract.

Keiyaku wo ichi nen enchō wo shite itadakitai no desu.

(kay-yah-kuu oh ee-chee nen en-choe oh shtay ee-tah-dah-kee tie no dess)

ex warehouse – *sōko watashi* (so-koe wah-tah-she)

ex works (factory) – *kōjō watashi* (koe-joe wah-tah-she)

— F —

face value – *gakumen kakaku* (gah-kuu-men kah-kah-kuu)

facilities – *setsubi* (say-t'sue-bee)

facsimile – *fakushimiri* (fah-kuu-she-mee-ree)

faction – *habatsu* (hah-bah-t'sue)

factionalism – *habatsu shugi* (hah-bah-t'sue shuu-ghee)

factor – *yōso* (yoe-so)

factory – *kōjō* (koe-joe)
Where is your factory located?
   Kōjō no basho wa doko desu ka?
   (koe-joe no bah-show wah doe-koe dess kah)

factory manager – *kōjō chō* (koe-joe choe)

factory overhead – *seizō kansetsu-hi* (say-zoe kahn-say-t'sue-he)

factory price – *kōjō watashi nedan* (koe-joe wah-tah-she nay-dahn)

factory worker – *kō in* (koe een)

fail – *shippai suru* (sheep-pie sue-rue); **failure** – *hasan* (hah-sahn)

fail (business) – *tōsan suru* (toe-sahn sue-rue)

fair – *kōsei* (koe-say); *seitō* (say-toe); **fair-minded** – *kōhei na* (koe-hay-nah)

fair market value – *kōsei shijō kakaku* (koe-say she-joe kah-kah-kuu)

fair return – *tekisei rieki* (tay-kee-say ree-ay-kee)

fair trade – *kōsei bōeki* (koe-say boe-ay-kee)

family – *kazoku* (kah-zoe-kuu)

family allowance – *kazoku teate* (kah-zoe-kuu tay-ah-tay)

farewell party – *sōbetsu kai* (so-bait-sue kye)

farmer – *nōmin* (no-mean)

farm out (send work out) – *gaichū suru* (guy-chew sue-rue)

fashion – *ryūkō* (r'yuu-koe); *fasshon* (fah-shone)

fast – *hayai* (hah-yie)

favorite bar – *iki-tsuke bā* (ee-kee-skay bah)
   Do you have a favorite bar?
   Iki-tsuke no bā ga arimasu ka?
   (ee-kee-skay no bah gah ah-ree-mahss-kah)

Federation of Economic Organizations (a key business group) – *Keidanren* (kay-dahn-ren)

fee; charge – *ryōkin* (rio-keen)
   How much is the fee?
   Ryōkin wa ikura desu ka?
   (rio-keen wah ee-kuu-rah dess kah)

feedback – *fiido bakku* (fee-doe bahk-kuu)

feel at ease – *anshin suru* (ahn-sheen sue-rue)

feeling; mood – *kimochi* (kee-moe-chee)
   I really feel good!
   Hontō ni kimochi ga ii desu!
   (hone-toe nee kee-moe-chee gah ee dess)

fender (auto) – *fenda* (fen-dah)

few – *sū* (sue); few people – *sū mei* (sue may)

fiber-optic communication – *hikari tsūshin* (he-kah-ree t'sue-sheen)

field warehousing – *itaku sōko gyōmu* (ee-tah-kuu so-koe g'yoe-muu)

figure; number – *sūji* (sue-jee)

file – *fairu* (fie-rue)

fill out (a form) – *kaki komu* (kah-kee koe-muu)

film – *firumu* (fee-rue-muu)

filter – *firuta* (fee-rue-tah)

finance – *yūshi suru* (yuu-she sue-rue)

finance company – *kin'yū gaisha* (keen-yuu guy-shah)

Finance Ministry – *Ōkurashō* (oh-kuu-rah-show)

financial – *zaimu* (zye-muu)

financial analysis – *zaimu bunseki* (zye-muu boon-say-kee)

financial appraisal – *zaimu satei* (zye-muu sah-tay)

financial control – *zaimu tōsei* (zye-muu toe-say)

financial crisis – *keizai no kiki* (kay-zye no kee-kee)

financial director – *zaimu kanrisha* (zye-muu kahn-ree-shah)

financial incentive – *zaimu yūin* (zye-muu yuu-een)

financial leverage – *fainansharu rebarejji* (fie-nahn-shah-rue ray-bah-ray-jee)

financial management – *zaimu kanri* (zye-muu kahn-ree)

financial period – *kaikei kikan* (kye-kay kee-kahn)
    When is your financial period?
        Anata no kaikei kikan wa itsu desu ka?
        (ah-nah-tah no kye-kay kee-kahn wah eat-sue dess kah)

financial planning – *zaimu keikaku* (zye-muu kay-kah-kuu)

financial services – *fainansharu sābisu* (fie-nahn-shah-rue sah-bee-sue)

financial statement – *zaimu shohyō* (zye-muu show-h'yoe)

financial year – *kaikei nendo* (kye-kay nen-doe)

financing (a loan) – *yūshi* (yuu-she)

finalize – *saishū-ka suru* (sigh-shuu-kah sue-rue)

fine (penalty) – *bakkin* (bahk-keen)

finished goods – *zaiko seihin* (zye-koe say-heen)

finished goods inventory – *zaiko seihin mokuroku* (zye-koe say-heen moe-kuu-roe-kuu)

fire (dismiss) – *kaiko suru* (kye-koe sue-rue)

firm (company) – *kaisha* (kye-shah)

firm stand – *tsuyoki* (t'sue-yoe-kee)

first (number one) – *ichibanme* (ee-chee-bahm-may)
first-class – *ichi-ryū* (ee-chee-r'yuu)
first-class company – *ichi-ryū gaisha* (ee-chee r'yuu guy-shah)
first-class school – *ichi-ryū kō* (ee-chee-r'yuu koe)
first-class ticket – *ittō no kippu* (eat-toe no keep-puu)
first edition – *sho han* (show hahn)
first ten days of the month – *jōjun* (joe-june)
first time – *hajimete* (hah-jee-may-tay); *saisho* (sigh-show)
  Is this your first time?
    Kore ga hajimete desu ka?
    (koe-ray gah hah-jee-may-tay dess kah)
first year – *ichinen me* (ee-chee-nen may)
fiscal agent – *zaimu dairiten* (zye-muu dye-ree-ten)
fiscal year – *kaikei nendo* (kye-kay nen-doe)
five percent discount – *go pāsento biki* (go pah-sen-toe bee-kee)
fix (repair) – *naosu* (nah-oh-sue); *naoseru* (nah-oh-say-rue)
fixed assets – *kotei shisan* (koe-tay she-sahn)
fixed capital – *kotei shihon* (koe-tay she-hone)
fixed charges (business) – *kakutei hi* (kah-kuu-tay he)
fixed costs; expenses – *kotei hi* (koe-tay he)
fixed investment – *kotei shihon tōshi* (koe-tay she-hone toe-she)
fixed liability – *kotei fusai* (koe-tay fuu-sigh)
fixed price – *teika* (tay-kah)
fixed rate of exchange – *kawase teiritsu* (kah-wah-say tay-ree-t'sue)
fixed term – *teiki* (tay-kee)
fixed terms – *kakutei jōken* (kah-kuu-tay joe-ken)
fix the price – *kakaku sōsa wo suru* (kah-kah-kuu so-sah oh sue-rue)
flat rate – *kin'itsu ryōkin* (keen-eat-sue rio-keen)

flat yield – *kin'itsu rimawari* (keen-eat-sue ree-mah-wah-ree)

flexible tariff – *shinshuku kanzei* (sheen-shuu-kuu kahn-zay)

flight number – *bin mei* (bean may); *furaito namba* (fuu-rye-toe-nahm-bah)

float (oustanding checks, stock) – *furōto* (fuu-roe-toe)

float (issue stock) – *kisai suru* (kee-sigh sue-rue)

floating asset – *ryūdō shisan* (r'yuu-doe she-sahn)

floating charge – *fudō tanpo* (fuu-doe tahm-poe)

floating debt – *ichiji kari-ire kin* (ee-chee-jee kah-ree-ee-ray keen)

floating exchange rate – *hendō kawase sōba* (hen-doe kah-wah-say so-bah)

floating exchange system – *hendō sōba sei* (hen-doe so-bah say)

floating rate – *jiyū hendō sōba* (jee-yuu hen-doe so-bah)

floor of stock exchange – *tachiai jō* (tah-chee-eye joe)

floppy disk – *furoppii disku* (fuu-roe-pee disk-uu)

flow chart – *gyōmu unkō-hyō* (g'yoe-muu uun-koe-h'yoe)

flow chart (production) – *seisan kōtei junjo ichiran-hyō* (say-sahn koe-tay june-joe ee-chee-rahn-h'yoe)

fluctuate (go up and down) – *age-sage* (ah-gay-sah-gay)

fluent – *ryūchō* (r'yuu-choe)

follower – *kobun* (koe-boon)

follow-up – *tsuiseki chōsa suru* (t'sue-ee-say-kee choe-sah sue-rue)

follow-up order – *oikake chūmon* (oh-ee-kah-kay chew-moan)

font (type style) – *fonto* (fone-toe)

food – *shokuji* (show-kuu-jee); main dish – *shushoku* (shuu-show-kuu); side dishes – *okazu* (oh-kah-zuu)

food processor – *fūdo purosessa* (fuu-doe pro-say-sah)
foodstuffs – *shokuryō* (show-kuu-rio)
forecast – *yosoku* (yoe-so-kuu); as expected – *yosō dōri* (yoe-so doe-ree); weather forecast – *tenki yohō* (ten-kee yoe-hoe)
forecast, to – *yosoku suru* (yoe-so-kuu sue-rue)
foreign (abroad, overseas) – *kaigai* (kye-guy)
foreign agent – *gaikoku dairiten* (guy-koe-kuu dye-ree-ten)
foreign bill of exchange – *gaikoku kawase tegata* (guy-koe-kuu kah-wah-say tay-gah-tah)
foreign company – *gaikoku gaisha* (guy-koe-kuu guy-shah)
foreign correspondent bank – *koruresu saki ginkō* (koe-rue-ray-sue sah-kee gheen-koe)
foreign currency – *gaika* (guy-kah)
foreign debt – *gaisai* (guy-sigh)
foreign demand – *gaiju* (guy-juu)
foreigner – *gaikoku-jin* (guy-koe-kuu-jeen)
foreign exchange – *gaikoku kawase* (guy-koe-kuu kah-wah-say)
foreign exchange bank – *gaikoku kawase ginko* (guy-koe-kuu kah-wah-say gheen-koe)
foreign exchange rate – *kawase sōba* (kah-wah-say so-bah)
foreign investment – *kaigai tōshi* (kye-guy toe-she)
foreign minister – *gai shō* (guy show)
Foreign Ministry – *Gaimushō* (guy-muu-show)
foreign securities – *gaikoku shōken* (guy-koe-kuu show-ken)
foreign tax credit – *gaikoku zeigaku kōjo* (guy-koe-kuu zay-gah-kuu koe-joe)
foreign trade – *gaikoku bōeki* (guy-koe-kuu boe-ay-kee)
foreman – *shoku-chō* (show-kuu-choe)

for export – *yushutsu yō* (yuu-shoot-sue yoe)

forgery – *gizō* (ghee-zoe)

forget – *wasureru* (wah-sue-ray-rue)

forgive – *yurusu* (yuu-rue-sue)

form (of printing layouts) – *kumiban* (kuu-me-bahn)

form (shape) – *katachi* (kah-tah-chee)

formalities, proceedings – *keshiki* (kay-she-kee); formalities (documents) – *tetsuzuki* (tay-t'sue-zuu-kee)

format (layout for printing) – *teisai* (tay-sigh)

form letter – *hinagata shokan* (hee-nah-gah-tah show-kahn)

formula (method) – *hōshiki* (hoe-she-kee)

forward contract – *sakimono keiyaku* (sah-kee-moe-no kay-yah-kuu)

forwarding agent – *unsō gyōsha* (uun-so g'yoe-shah)

forward margin – *sakimono mājin* (sah-kee-moe-no mah-jeen)

forward market – *sakimono shijō* (sah-kee-moe-no she-joe)

forward purchase – *sakimono kaitsuke* (sah-kee-moe-no kite-sue-kay)

forward shipment – *saki tsumidashi* (sah-kee t'sue-me-dah-she)

foundation; basis – *kiso* (kee-so)

four colors (as in four-color printing) – *yon shoku zuri* (yoan show-kuu zuu-ree)

four-wheel drive – *yonrin kudō* (yoan-reen kuu-doe)

franchise – *itte hanbai* (eat-tay hahn-by)

franchise (sales) – *itte hanbai ken* (eat-tay hahn-by ken)

fraud (swindle) – *sagi* (sah-ghee)

free (of charge) – *muryō* (muu-rio)

This sample is free.

  Kono mihon wa muryō desu.

  (koe-no me-hone wah muu-rio dess)

free alongside ship – *sensoku watashi* (sen-so-kuu wah-tah-she)

free and clear – *teitō ni haitte inai* (tay-toe nee height-tay ee-nigh)

free enterprise – *jiyū kigyō* (jee-yuu kee-g'yoe)

freelancer – *jiyū-gyō* (jee-yuu g'yoe)

free list (commodities without customs duty) – *menzei hin mokuroku* (men-zay heen moe-kuu-roe-kuu)

free market – *jiyū shijō* (jee-yuu she-joe)

free on board – *honsen watashi* (hone-sen wah-tah-she)

free on rail – *kasha watashi* (kah-shah wah-tah-she)

free port – *jiyū bōeki kō* (jee-yuu boe-ay-kee koe)

free time – *jiyū jikan* (jee-yuu jee-kahn)

free trade – *jiyū bōeki* (jee-yuu boe-ay-kee)

free trade zone – *jiyū bōeki ken* (jee-yuu boe-ay-kee ken)

freight – *kamotsu* (kah-moat-sue)

freight collect – *unchin tōchakuchi barai* (uun-cheen toe-chah-kuu-chee bah-rye)

freighter (vessel) – *kamotsu-sen* (kah-moat-sue-sen)
On what day will the freighter arrive?
Kamotsu-sen wa nan nichi ni tōchaku shimasu ka? (kah-moat-sue-sen wah nahn nee-chee nee toe-chah-kuu she-mahss kah)

freight forwarder – *kamotsu toriatsukai gyōsha* (kah-moat-sue toe-ree-ah-t'sue-kye g'yoe-shah)

freight included – *unchin komi* (uun-cheen koe-me)

freight insurance – *unchin hoken* (uun-cheen hoe-ken)

freight prepaid – *unchin mae barai* (uun-cheen my bah-rye)

fringe benefits – *fuka kyūfu* (fuu-kah cue-fuu)

fringe market – *niji-teki shijō* (nee-jee-tay-kee she-joe)

front-end fee – *shinjikēto sosei sho hiyō* (sheen-jee-kay-toe so-say show h'yoe)

front-wheel drive – *zenrin kudō* (zen-reen kuu-doe)

frozen assets – *tōketsu shisan* (toe-kate-sue she-sahn)

fuel (for combustion engines) – *nenryō* (nen-rio)

fuel consumption – *nenryō shōhiryō* (nen-rio show-hee-rio)

full page "bleed" ad – *tachikiri* (tah-chee-kee-ree)

full scale – *honkaku teki* (hone-kah-kuu tay-kee)

full settlement – *sō kessan* (so case-sahn)

functional analysis – *kinō bunseki* (kee-no boon-say-kee)

funds (capital) – *shikin* (she-keen); *shihonkin* (she-hone-keen)

futures (finance) – *sakimono torihiki* (sah-kee-moe-no toe-ree-hee-kee)

futures (securities) – *sakimono keiyaku* (sah-kee-moe-no kay-yah-kuu)

futures option – *sakimono opushon* (sah-kee-moe-no op-shone)

— G —

gap – *hiraki* (he-rah-kee); *gyappu* (gahp-puu)

garnishment – *sashiosae* (sah-she-oh-sigh)

gas – *gasu* (gah-sue)

gasoline – *gasorin* (gah-so-reen)

gas peddle – *akuseru* (ah-kuu-say-rue)

gas tank – *gasu tanku* (gah-sue tahn-kuu)

gearshift – *gia tenkan sōchi* (ghee-ah ten-kahn so-chee)

general; generally (in a general sense) – *ippan* (ee-pahn); in most cases – *taitei* (tie-tay)
   I generally get up at six o'clock every morning.
   Taitei mai asa rokuji ni okimasu.
   (tie-tay my ah-sah roe-kuu-jee nee oh-kee-mahss)

general acceptance – *futsū hikiuke* (fuu-t'sue he-kee-uu-kay)

general affairs (business) – *sōmu* (so-muu)

general affairs department of a company – *sōmu bu* (so-muu buu)
   I have an appointment with the manager of the general affairs department.
   Sōmu bu no buchō to yakusoku ga arimasu.
   (so-muu buu no buu-choe toe yahk-so-kuu gah ah-ree-mahss)

general manager – *sō shihainin* (so she-high-neen)

general meeting – *sōkai* (so-kye)

general partnership company – *gōmei gaisha* (go-may guy-shah)

general shareholders' meeting – *kabunushi sōkai* (kah-buu-nuu-she so-kye)

general strike – *zenesuto* (zay-nay-sue-toe)

generator (for electricity) – *jenerēta* (jay-nay-ray-tah)

gentleman's agreement – *shinshi kyōtei* (sheen-she k'yoe-tay)

A gentleman's agreement will be fine.

Shinshi kyōtei wa daijōbu desu.

(sheen-she k'yoe-tay wah dye-joe-buu dess)

gift (present) – *omiyage* (oh-me-yah-gay); *okurimono* (oh-kuu-ree-moe-no); *gifuto* (gift-oh)

Thank you very much for the gift.

Omiyage wo dōmo arigatō gozaimashita.

(oh-me-yah-gay oh doe-moe ah-ree-gah-toe go-zye-mah-shtah)

glossy (photo on coated paper) – *tsuya dashi no* (t'sue-yah dah-she no)

glut (excess) – *kyōkyū kajō* (k'yoe-cue kah-joe)

go-between in business – *chūkai-nin* (chew-kye-neen)

I am looking for a go-between.

Chūkai-nin wo sagashite imasu.

(chew-kye-neen oh sah-gah-shtay ee-mahss)

godown (warehouse) – *sōko* (so-koe)

go down (decrease) – *sagaru* (sah-gah-rue)

going rate (price) – *genkō buai* (gen-koe buu-eye)

golf – *gorufu* (go-rue-fuu); have a passion for golf – *gorufu-zuki* (go-rue-fuu-zuu-kee)

good luck – *kōun* (koe-uun)

good-luck day – *tai-an* (tie ahn)

goods (merchandise) – *busshi* (boosh-she); *shōhin* (show-heen)

goods, capital – *shihon zai* (she-hone zye)

goods, consumer – *shōhi zai* (show-hee zye)

goods, durable – *taikyū zai* (tie-cue zye)

goods, industrial – *seisan shizai* (say-sahn she-zye)

goods in stock – *zaikobun* (zye-koe-boon)

good weather – *ii tenki* (ee ten-kee)

goodwill (with customers) – *eigyō ken* (ay-g'yoe ken)

go public with stock – *kabushiki kōkai suru* (kah-buu-she-kee koe-kye sue-rue)

go to meet – *mukae ni iku* (muu-kye nee ee-kuu)
Don't worry. I will (go to) meet you.
    Go-shimpai wa irimasen. O-mukae ni ikimasu.
    (go-sheem-pie wah ee-ree-mah-sen oh-muu-kye nee ee-kee-mahss)

government – *seifu* (say-fuu); Japanese government – *Nihon seifu* (nee-hone say-fuu)

government agency – *seifu kikan* (say-fuu kee-kahn)

government bank (central bank) – *Chuo Ginkō* (chew-oh gheen-koe)

government bonds – *koku sai* (coke sigh)

government leader – *seifu no shidō sha* (say-fuu no she-doe sha)

government policy – *seifu no seisaku* (say-fuu no say-sah-kuu)
Do you always follow government policy?
    Seifu no seisaku ni itsumo shitagaimasu ka?
    (say-fuu no say-sah-kuu nee eat-sue-moe shtah-guy-mahss kah)

grace period – *yūyo kikan* (yuu-yoe kee-kahn)

grade, commercial – *shōgyō kakuzuke* (show-g'yoe kah-kuu-zuu-kay)

grade (stage) – *dankai* (dahn-kye)

graft – *shūwai* (shuu-why)

grain – *kokumotsu* (koe-kuu-moat-sue)

grain (of photo or piece of art or film) – *kime* (kee-may)

graph – *gurafu* (guu-rah-fuu)

gratuity (tip) – *chippu* (cheap-puu)
Is it necessary to tip here?
    Koko de chippu ga irimasu ka?
    (koe-koe day cheap-puu gah ee-ree-mahss kah)

gray market – *gurei māketto* (guu-ray mah-ket-toe)

great number (majority) – *tasū* (tah-sue)

greetings (greeting visitors in your office or visiting someone's office and greeting them is a very important part of Japanese protocol) – *aisatsu* (eye-sah-t'sue)

grievance procedure – *kujō shori tetsuzuki* (kuu-joe show-ree tay-t'sue-zuu-kee)

gross income – *sō shotoku* (so show-toe-kuu)

gross investment – *sō tōshi* (so toe-she)

gross loss – *sō sonshitsu* (so soan-sheet-sue)

gross margin – *sō rieki* (so ree-ay-kee)

gross national product – *kokumin sō seisan* (koe-kuu-meen so say-sahn)

gross profit – *sō rieki* (so ree-ay-kee)

gross sales – *sō uriage daka* (so uu-ree-ah-gay dah-kah)

gross spread – *ne zaya* (nay zah-yah)

gross weight – *sō jūryō* (so juu-rio)

gross yield – *sō rimawari* (so ree-mah-wah-ree)

ground (earth) – *jimen* (jee-men)

group accounts – *gurūpu kanjō* (guu-ruu-puu kahn-joe)

group discussion – *hanashiai* (hah-nah-she-eye)

group dynamics – *gurūpu dainamikkusu* (guu-ruu-puu dye-nah-meek-sue)

group insurance – *dantai hoken* (dahn-tie hoe-ken)

group spirit – *shūdan ishiki* (shuu-dahn ee-she-kee)

group training – *shūdan kunren* (shuu-dahn coon-ren)

grow; raise (crop) – *saibai suru* (sigh-by sue-rue)
  Are soybeans raised in Japan?
    Nihon de daizu wo saibai shite imasu ka?
    (nee-hone day dye-zuu oh sigh-by shtay ee-mahss kah)

grow; raise (child) – *sodatsu* (so-dah-t'sue)
  Where were you raised?

Doko de sodachimashita ka?
(doe-koe day so-dah-chee-mahsh-tah kah)

growth – *seichō (say-choe)*

growth, corporate – *kigyō seichō* (kee-g'yoe say-choe)

growth index – *seichō shisū* (say-choe she-sue)

growth industry – *seichō sangyō* (say-choe sahng-g'yoe)

growth potential – *seichō no kanōsei* (say-choe no kah-no-say)
Do you think this has growth potential?
Kore wa seichō no kanōsei ga aru to omoimasu ka?
(koe-ray wah say-choe no kah-no-say gah ah-rue toe oh-moe-ee-mahss kah)

growth rate – *seichō ritsu* (say-choe ree-t'sue)

growth stock – *seichō kabu* (say-choe kah-buu)

guarantee – *hoshō shimasu* (hoe-show she-mahss)
I will guarantee payment.
Shiharai wo hoshō shimasu.
(she-hah-rye oh hoe-show she-mahss)

guarantee deposit/payment – *hoshō kin* (hoe-show keen)

guaranteed salary – *kotei kyū* (koe-tay cue)

guaranty bond – *hoshō sho* (hoe-show show)

guaranty company – *hoshō gaisha* (hoe-show guy-shah)

guess – *suisatsu* (sue-ee-saht-sue); *ate zuiryō* (ah-tay zuu-ee-rio)

guide (lead) – *annai* (ahn-nigh); *annai suru* (ahn-nigh sue-rue)

guidelines – *gaido rain* (guy-doe rine)

— H —

half – *hanbun* (hahn-boon)
Just half will be enough.
   Hanbun de jūbun desu.
   (hahn-boon day juu-boon dess)

half a year – *hantoshi* (hahn toe-she)
I have been in Japan for half a year.
   Hantoshi Nihon ni imasu.
   (hahn-toe-she nee-hone nee ee-mahss)

half-finished goods – *han-sei hin* (hahn-say heen)

hand-clapping (to mark an auspicious event) – *te-jime* (tay-jee-may)

handicap – *furi na jōken* (fuu-ree nah joe-ken)

handling – *tori atsukai* (toe-ree ah-t'sue-kye)

handling charge – *tesūryō* (tay-sue-rio)
About how much will the handling charge be?
   Tesūryō wa daitai ikura ni narimasu ka?
   (tay-sue-rio wah dye-tie ee-kuu-rah nee nah-ree-mahss kah)

hand-made – *te-zukuri no* (tay-zuu-kuu-ree no)

hand-painted – *te-nuri no* (tay-nuu-ree no)

Haneda Airport – *Haneda Kūkō* (hah-nay-dah kuu-koe)

hard (to the touch) – *katai* (kah-tie); difficult – *muzukashii* (muu-zuu-kah-she)
This work is very difficult.
   Kono shigoto wa taihen muzukashii desu.
   (koe-no she-go-toe wah tie-hen muu-zuu-kah-she dess)

hard copy – *hādo kopii* (hah-doe koe-pee)
I need hard copy too.
   Hādo kopii mo irimasu.

(hah-doe koe-pee moe ee-ree-mahss)

hardcover (as in book) – *hādo kabā* (hah-doe kah-bah); *kata byōshi bon* (kah-tah b'yoe-she bone)

hard currency – *kōkan kanō tsūka* (koe-kahn kah-no t'sue-kah)

hard sell – *hādo sēru* (hah-doe say-rue)

hardware – *hādo wea* (hah-doe way-ah)

harmony – *wa* (wah)

headhunter (new employee scout) – *jinzai sukauto* (jeen-zye scout-oh)

headline – *midashi* (me-dah-she); *heddo rain* (hay-doe rine)

This headline is meaningless.

Kono midashi wa imi ga nai.

(koe-no me-dah-she wah ee-me gah nigh)

head office – *honsha* (hone-shah)

(Our) head office has moved to Shinjuku.

Honsha wa Shinjuku ni utsurimashita.

(hone-shah wah sheen-juu-kuu nee uu-t'sue-ree-mah-shtah)

headquarters – *honbu* (hone-buu)

heavy – *omoi* (oh-moy)

heavy industry – *jū kōgyō* (juu koe-g'yoe)

heavy labor – *chikara shigoto* (chee-kah-rah she-go-toe)

I am not used to heavy labor/work.

Chikara shigoto ni narete imasen.

(chee-kah-rah she-go-toe nee nah-ray-tay ee-mah-sen)

hectare (2.471 acres) – *hekutāru* (hay-kuu-tah-rue)

hedge (one's position) – *tsunagu* (t'sue-nah-guu)

help (care) – *o-sewa* (oh-say-wah)

Thanks for your help.

O-sewa ni natte imasu.

(oh-say-wah nee nah-tay ee-mahss)

help wanted (advertisement) – *kyūjin* (cue-jeen)

hidden assets – *intoku shisan* (een-toe-kuu she-sahn)

hidden assets (securities) – *fukumi shisan* (fuu-kuu-me she-sahn)

high – *takai* (tah-kye)

high fidelity – *haifai* (high-fie)

high quality – *yūshū na* (yuu-shuu nah)

high technology – *haiteku* (high-tay-kuu)

high tech product – *haiteku seihin* (high-take-kuu say-heen)

high yen – *en daka* (en dah-kah)

highest bidder – *saikō nyūsatsu-nin* (sigh-koe n'yuu-sah-t'sue-neen)

   Who was the highest bidder?

     Saikō nyūsatsu-nin wa donata deshita ka?

     (sigh-koe n'yuu-sah-t'sue-neen wa doe-nah-tah desh-tah kah)

hobby – *shumi* (shuu-me)

holding company – *mochikabu gaisha* (moe-chee-kah-buu guy-shah)

   Who is president of your holding company?

     Anata no mochikabu gaisha no shachō wa donata desu ka?

     (ah-nah-tah no moe-chee-kah-buu guy-shah no shah-choe wah doe-nah-tah dess kah)

holding period – *horyū kikan* (hoe-r'yuu kee-kahn)

holiday (day off) – *yasumi* (yah-sue-me); take a day or days off – *yasumi wo toru* (yah-sue-me oh toe-rue)

home market – *kokunai shijō* (koe-kuu-nigh she-joe)

hope – *mikomi* (me-koe-me); hope (yours) – *go-kibo* (go-kee-boe)

horsepower – *bariki* (bah-ree-kee)

hostess (in cabaret, etc.) – *hosutesu* (hoe-stay-sue)

hot – *atsui* (ah-t'sue-ee)

hot money – *hotto mane* (hoe-toe mah-nay)

hourly earnings – *jikan shū* (jee-kahn-shuu)

hourly pay – *jikan kyū* (jee-kahn cue)

hours of operation – *kadō jikan* (kah-doe jee-kahn);
 eigyō jikan (egg-yoe jee-kahn)
 What are the business hours of Mitsukoshi Department Store?
  *Mitsukoshi Depāto no eigyō jikan wa nanji kara
  nanji made desu ka?*
  (meet-sue-koe-she day-pah-toe no egg-yoe jee-kahn
  wah nahn-jee kah-rah nan-jee mah-day dess kah)

household – *shotai* (show-tie)

House of Councillors – *Sangi-in* (sahn-ghee-een);
 councillor – *Sangi-in giin* (sahn-ghee-een ghee-een)

House of Representatives – *Shūgi-in* (shuu-ghee-
 een); representative – *Shūgi-in giin* (shuu-ghee-een
 ghee-een)

house phone – *hausu fon* (how-sue phone)
 Where are the house phones?
  Hausu fon wa doko desu ka?
  (how-sue phone wah doe-koe dess kah)

human resources – *jinteki shigen* (jeen-tay-kee she-
 gen)

human rights – *jin ken* (jeen ken)

hybrid materials – *haiburiddo zairyō* (high-buu-reed-
 doe zye-rio)

hygiene; sanitation – *eisei* (ay-say)

— I —

idea (thought) – *kangae* (kahn-guy)
  That is really a good idea.
   Sore wa hontō ni ii kangae desu.
   (so-ray wah hone-toe nee ee kahn-guy dess)
ideal – *risō* (ree-so); ideally – *risō to shite* (ree-so toe shtay)
identification (I.D.) – *mibun shōmei sho* (me-boon show-may show)
  Please let me see some identification.
   Mibun shōmei sho wo misete kudasai.
   (me-boon show-may show oh me-say-tay kuu-dah-sigh)
idle capacity (facilities) – *yūkyū shisetsu* (yuu-cue she-say-t'sue)
ignition – *igunisshon* (ee-guu-nee-shone)
ignore (disregard) – *mushi suru* (muu-she sue-rue)
illegal – *fuhō-no* (fuu-hoe-no)
illegal shipments – *ihō no funazumi* (ee-hoe no fuu-nah-zuu-me)
illustration – *irasuto* (ee-rah-stow)
imagination – *sōzō* (so-zoe)
imitation product – *mōzō hin* (moe-zoe heen);
  nisemono (nee-say-moe-no)
  This looks like an imitation.
   Kore wa nisemono no yō desu.
   (koe-ray wah nee-say-moe-no no yoe dess)
immediately! – *dai-shikyū!* (dye-she-cue)
impatient – *sekkachi na* (sake-kah-chee nah)
impending changes – *sashisematta henka* (sah-she-say-maht-tah hen-kah)
implied agreement – *moku daku* (moe-kuu dah-kuu)

import – *yunyū* (yuun-yuu)
import, to – *yunyū suru* (yuun-yuu sue-rue)
What kind of merchandise do you import?
> *Donna shinamono wo yunyū shite imasu ka?*
> (doan-nah she-nah-moe-no oh yuun-yuu shtay ee-mahss kah)

important – *jūdai* (juu-dye)
important point – *jūten* (juu-ten)
import company – *yunyū gyōsha* (yuun-yuu g'yoe-shah)
import declaration – *yunyū shinkoku* (yuun-yuu sheen-koe-kuu)
import deposit – *yunyū tanpo* (yuun-yuu tahn-poe)
import duty – *yunyū kanzei* (yuun-yuu kahn-zay)
import entry – *yunyū tetsuzuki* (yuun-yuu tay-t'sue-zuu-kee)
importer – *yunyū-shō* (yuun-yuu-show)
import license/permit – *yunyū kyoka* (yuun-yuu k'yoe-kah)
import quota – *yunyū wariate* (yuun-yuu wah-ree-ah-tay)
Does Japan have an import quota for Western-style wearing apparel?
> *Nihon wa yōfuku no yunyū wariate ga arimasu ka?*
> (nee-hone wah yoe-fuu-kuu no yuun-yuu wah-ree-ah-tay gah ah-ree-mahss kah)

How much did the percentage rise for import quota?
> *Yunyū wariate wa nan pāsento appu desu ka?*
> (yuun-yuu wah-ree-ah-tay wah nahn pah-cent-oh up dess kah)

import regulations – *yunyū kisoku* (yuun-yuu kee-so-kuu)
import tariff (list) – *yunyū kanzei-hyō* (yuun-yuu kahn-zay-h'yoe)

import tariffs – *yunyū zeiritsu* (yuun-yuu zay-ree-t'sue)

import tax – *yunyū zei* (yuun-yuu zay)

impound – *sashi osaeru* (sah-she oh-sigh-rue)

impressed; impressive – *kandō suru* (kahn-doe sue-rue); *kanshin* (kahn-sheen)

    I was very impressed with Mr. Obata.
        Obata-san ni taihen kanshin shimashita.
        (oh-bah-tah-san nee tie-hen kahn-sheen she-mah-shtah)

impression – *inshō* (en-show); first impression – *dai-ichi inshō* (dye-ee-chee een-show)

improvement – *kaizen* (kye-zen)

impulse buying – *shōdō gai* (show-doe guy)

in addition to (besides) – *hoka ni* (hoe-kah nee)

    Do you have any sizes besides this?
        Kono saizu no hoka ni saizu ga arimasu ka?
        (koe-no sigh-zuu no hoe-kah nee sigh-zuu gah ah-ree-mahss kah)

inadequate – *futekisetsu na* (fuu-tay-kee-say-t'sue nah)

in advance – *maemotte* (my-moat-tay); advance payment – *uchi kin* (uu-chee keen)

incentive – *yūin* (yuu-een)

    He will not move without an incentive.
        Yūin ga nahattara kare wa ugokimasen.
        (yu-een gah nah-kah-tah-rah kah-ray wah uu-go-kee-mah-sen)

incidental expenses – *rinji hi* (reen-jee hee)

include – *fukumu* (fuu-kuu-muu)

income – *shotoku* (show-toe-kuu); *shūnyū* (shuun-yuu); gross income – *sō shūnyū* (so shuun-yuu); net income – *jun shotoku* (june show-toe-kuu)

income bracket – *shotoku kaisō* (show-toe-koe kye-so)

income statement – *shotoku keisan sho* (show-toe-kuu kay-sahn show)

income tax – *shotoku zei* (show-toe-kuu zay)

income tax, corporate – *hōjin zei* (hoe-jeen zay)

income tax, personal – *kojin shotoku zei* (koe-jeen show-toe-kuu zay)

income yield – *shūeki rimawari* (shuu-ay-kee ree-mah-wah-ree)

inconstant – *kawari yasui* (kah-wah-ree yah-sue-ee)

incorporate – *kabushiki gaisha ni suru* (kah-buu-she-kee guy-shah nee sue-rue)

increase – *fueru* (fuu-ay-rue); *fuyasu* (fuu-yah-sue)

increase (in business, population, weight) – *zōka* (zoe-kah)

increase, to – *zōka suru* (zoe-kah sue-rue)

incremental cash flow – *zōka kyasshu furō* (zoe-kah k'yah-shuu fuu-roe)

indebtedness – *fusai* (fuu-sigh)

indemnity – *hoshō* (hoe-show)

independent (self-supporting) – *dokuritsu* (doe-kuu-ree-t'sue)

independent suspension – *dokuritsu kenka* (doe-kuu-ree-t'sue ken-kah)

index (indicator) – *shisū* (she-sue)

index, to – *sakuin wo tsukeru* (sah-kuu-een oh skay-rue)

indexing – *bukka suraido sei* (buu-kah sue-rye-doe say)

indirect claim – *kansetsu yōkyū* (kahn-say-t'sue yoe-cue)

indirect cost – *kansetsu hi* (kahn-say-t'sue hee)

indirect expenses – *kansetsu keihi* (kahn-say-t'sue kay-he); *kansetsu hi* (kahn-say-t'sue he)
Indirect expenses are eating into our profits.
Kansetsu hi wa zōdai rieki wo appaku shiteimasu.

(kahn-say-t'sue wah no zoe-dye ree-ay-kee oh ah-pah-kuu shtay-ee-mahss)

indirect labor – *kansetsu rōdō* (kahn-say-t'sue roe-doe)

indirect tax – *kansetsu zei* (kahn-say-t'sue zay)

individual – *kojin* (koe-jeen)
   He is the type who prefers to work by himself.
      Ano hito wa kojin de hatarakitai taipu desu.
      (ah-no shtoe wah koe-jeen day hah-tah-rah-kee-tie tie-puu dess)

individualism – *kojin-shugi* (koe-jeen-shuu-ghee)

industrial – *sangyō* (sahn-g'yoe); *kōgyō* (koe-g'yoe)

industrial accidents – *rōmu saigai* (roe-muu sigh-guy)

industrial arbitration – *rōdō chōtei* (roe-doe choe-tay)

industrial goods – *seisan shizai* (say-sahn she-zye)

industrialist – *kōgyōka* (koe-g'yoe-kah)

industrial insurance – *kan-i hoken* (kah-nee hoe-ken)

industrial park – *kōgyō danchi* (koe-g'yoe dahn-chee)
   Is your factory in an industrial park?
      Anata no kōjō wa kōgyō danchi ni arimasu ka?
      (ah-nah-tah no koe-joe wah koe-g'yoe dahn-chee nee ah-ree-mahss kah)

industrial planning – *sangyō keikaku* (sahn-g'yoe kay-kah-kuu)

industrial relations – *rōshi kankei* (roe-she kahn-kay)

industrial robot – *sangyō robotto* (sahn-g'yoe roe-boat-toe)

industrial union – *sangyō-betsu rōdō-kumiai* (sahn-g'yoe-bay-t'sue roe-doe-kuu-me-eye)

industry – *sangyō* (sahn-g'yoe)

industrywide – *sangyō zentai no* (sahn-g'yoe zen-tie no)

inefficient – *hi nōritsuteki na* (he-no-reet-stay-kee nah)

inexperience – *mu-keiken* (muu-kay-ken)

The new man is completely inexperienced.

Atarashii hito wa mattaku mu-keiken desu.

(ah-tah-rah-she shtoe wah mah-tah-kuu muu-kay-ken dess)

inferior parts – *furyō buhin* (fuu-rio buu-heen)

inflation – *infure* (een-fuu-ray)

inflationary – *infure no* (een-fuu-ray no)

influence – *eikyō* (ay-k'yoe)

influential – *yūryoku* (yuu-rio-kuu)

inform (notify) – *shiraseru* (she-rah-say-rue)

I will notify you tomorrow.

Ashita shirasemasu.

(ah-shtah she-rah-say-mahss)

information (report) – *jōhō* (joe-hoe), *hōdō* (hoe-doe)

information desk/counter – *annai jo* (ahn-nigh joe); *uketsuke* (uu-kate-sue-kay)

Please ask at the information desk.

Uketsuke de kiite kudasai.

(uu-kate-sue-kay day kee-tay kuu-dah-sigh)

infrared – *sekigai* (say-kee-guy)

infrastructure (economic) – *keizai kiban* (kay-zye kee-bahn)

infringement – *ihan* (ee-hahn)

inheritance – *sōzoku* (so-zoe-kuu)

inheritance tax – *isan sōzoku zei* (ee-sahn so-zoe-kuu zay)

injunction – *kyōsei meirei* (k'yoe-say may-ray)

ink – *inku* (een-kuu)

inland bill of lading – *kokunai funani shōken* (koe-kuu-nigh fuu-nah-nee show-ken)

innovation – *gijutsu kakushin* (ghee-jute-sue kah-kuu-sheen)

input – *inputto* (een-pute-toe)

inquiry – *hankyō* (hahn-k'yoe); *toiawase* (toe-ee-ah-wah-say); *kikiawase* (kee-kee-ah-wah-say)
  We receive more than one hundred inquiries every day.
> *Mainichi hyaku ijō no hankyō ga arimasu.*
> (my-nee-chee h'yah-kuu ee-joe no hahn-k'yoe gah ah-ree-mahss)

insert (as used in printing) – *sōnyū* (soan-yuu); *sashikomi* (sah-she-koe-me)

inside – *uchigawa* (uu-chee-gah-wah); *naimen* (nigh-men)

inside cover of magazine – *naka byōshi* (nah-kah b'yoe-she)

insolvent (company or person) – *shiharai funōsha* (she-hah-rye fuu-no-shah)

inspect (check) – *kensa suru* (ken-sah sue-rue); inspection – *tenken* (ten-ken)
  I must inspect this baggage.
> *Kono nimotsu wo kensa shinakereba narimasen.*
> (koh-no nee-moat-sue oh ken-sah she-nah-kay-ray-bah nah-ree-mah-sen)

inspector – *kensa-kan* (ken-sah-kahn)

instability – *fuantei* (fuu-ahn-tay)

install (equipment or something) – *toritsukeru* (toe-ree-t'sue-kay-rue); installation – *fusetsu* (fuu-say t'sue); installation cost – *fusetsu hi* (fuu-say-t'sue he)

installment credit – *fubarai shin'yō* (fuu-bah-rye sheen-yoe)

installment plan – *bunkatsu shiharai hōshiki* (boon-kah-t'sue she-hah-rye hoe-she-kee)

institutional advertising – *kigyō kōkoku* (kee-g'yoe koe-koe-kuu)

institutional investor – *kikan tōshi ka* (kee-kahn toe-she kah)

instruction – *sashizu* (sah-she-zoo); instruction manual – *kaisetsu sho* (kye-sate-sue show)

insurance – *hoken* (hoe-ken)

Do you have insurance?

Hoken ga arimasu ka?

(hoe-ken gah ah-ree-mahss kah)

insurance company – *hoken gaisha* (hoe-ken guy-shah)

insurance fund – *hoken tsumitate-kin* (hoe-ken t'sue-me-tah-tay-keen)

insurance policy – *hoken shōken* (hoe-ken show-ken)

insurance premium – *hoken ryō* (hoe-ken rio)

insurance underwriter – *hoken gyōsha* (hoe-ken g'yoe-shah)

insure – *hoken wo tsukeru* (hoe-ken oh t'sue-kay-rue)

intangible assets – *mukei shisan* (muu-kay she-sahn)

integrate – *sōgō suru* (so-go sue-rue)

integrated circuit – *shūseki kairo* (shuu-say-kee kye-roe)

intelligence – *chinō* (chee-no)

intelligent robot – *chinō robotto* (chee-no roe-boat-toe)

interbank – *ginkō-kan no* (gheen-koe-kahn no)

interchangeable lenses – *kōkan renzu* (koe-kahn ren-zuu)

interest (profit) – *risoku* (ree-so-kuu); interest rate – *kinri* (keen-ree); interest yield – *rimawari* (ree-mah-wah-ree)

interest – *rishi* (ree-she)

interest compounded – *fukuri* (fuu-kuu-ree)

interest income – *rishi shotoku* (ree-she show-toe-kuu)

interest period – *kinri kikan* (keen-ree kee-kahn)

interest rate – *riritsu* (ree-ree-t'sue)

What is the interest rate?

Riritsu wa nan desu ka?

(ree-ree-t'sue wah nahn dess kah)

interface – *intāfēsu* (een-tah-fay-sue)

interim budget – *zantei yosan* (zahn-tay yoe-sahn)

interim – *kari no* (kah-ree no)

interim statement – *kari keisan sho* (kah-ree kay-sahn show)

interlocking directorate – *kennin jūyaku* (ken-neen juu-yah-kuu)

intermediary – *chūkai sha* (chew-kye shah)

internal (inside a company) – *naibu no* (nigh-buu no)

internal (domestic) – *kokunai* (koe-kuu-nigh)

internal audit – *naibu kansa* (nigh-buu kahn-sah)

internal finance – *jiko kin'yū* (jee-koe keen-yuu)

internal rate of return – *naibu shūeki ritsu* (nigh-buu shuu-ay-kee ree-t'sue)

internal revenue tax – *naikoku shūnyū zei* (nigh-koe-kuu shuun-yuu zay)

international – *kokusai* (coke-sigh)

international date line – *kokusai hizuke henkō-sen* (coke-sigh he-zuu-kay hen-koe-sen)

international driver's license – *kokusai unten menkyo shō* (coke-sigh uun-ten men-k'yoe show)

Do you have an international driver's license?

Kokusai unten menkyo shō wo motte imasu ka? (coke-sigh uun-ten men-k'yoe show oh moat-tay ee-mahss kah)

internationalize – *kokusai-ka* (coke-sigh-kah)

interpretation – *kaishaku* (kye-shah-kuu)

interpreter – *tsūyaku* (t'sue-yah-kuu)

Please call an interpreter.

Tsūyaku wo yonde kudasai. (t'sue-yah-kuu oh yoan-day kuu-dah-sigh)

interruption – *teishi* (tay-she)

inter-state commerce – *shū-kan tsūshō* (shuu-kahn t'sue-show)

interview – *kaiken* (kye-ken); *intabyū* (een-tah-b'yuu); (for story) – *menkai* (main-kye); for employment – *mensetsu* (men-say-t'sue)

in the red – *akaji de* (ah-kah-jee day)

in transit – *unsō chū* (uun-so chew)

intrinsic value – *honshitsu kachi* (hone-sheet-sue kah-chee)

introduce – *shōkai suru* (show-kye sue-rue)
  I will introduce you to Mr. Smith.
    Sumisu-san ni shōkai shimasu
    (sue-mee-sue-sahn nee show-kye she-mahss)

introduction (in book) – *jo* (joe)

invalidate – *mukō ni suru* (muu-koe nee sue-rue)

invent – *hatsumei suru* (hot-sue-may sue-rue)
  It was invented last year.
    Kyonen hatsumei shimashita.
    (k'yoe-nen hot-sue-may she-mah-shtah)

invention – *hatsumei* (hot-sue-may)

inventor – *hatsumeika* (hot-sue-may-kah)
  Do you know the name of the inventor?
    Hatsumeika no namae wo shitte imasu ka?
    (hot-sue-may-kah no nah-my oh sheet-tay ee-mahss kah)

inventory – *zaiko hin* (zye-koe heen)

inventory control – *zaiko hin kanri* (zye-koe heen kahn-ree)

inventory turnover – *tana oroshi shisan kaiten ritsu* (tah-nah oh-roe-she she-sahn kye-ten ree-t'sue)

invest – *tōshi suru* (toe-she sue-rue)

invested capital – *tōka shihon* (toe-kah she-hone)

investigation, inquiry – *chōsa* (choe-sah); *torishirabe* (toe-ree-she-rah-bay)

investment – *tōshi* (toe-she)

investment analysis – *tōshi bunseki* (toe-she boon-say-kee)

investment appraisal – *tōshi satei* (toe-she sah-tay)

investment bank – *tōshi ginkō* (toe-she gheen-koe)

investment budget – *tōshi yosan* (toe-she yoe-sahn)

investment company – *tōshi shintaku gaisha* (toe-she sheen-tah-kuu guy-shah)

investment criteria – *tōshi kijun* (toe-she kee-june)

investment fund – *tōshi shintaku* (toe-she sheen-tah-kuu)

investment policy – *tōshi seisaku* (toe-she say-sah-kuu)

investment program – *tōshi keikaku* (toe-she kay-kah-kuu)

investment return – *tōshi rimawari* (toe-she ree-mah-wah-ree)

investment strategy – *tōshi senryaku* (toe-she sen-r'yah-kuu)

investment trust – *tōshi shintaku* (toe-she sheen-tah-kuu)

invitation to bid – *nyūsatsu kan'yū* (n'yuu-sah-t'sue kahn-yuu)

invite – *shōtai suru* (show-tie sue-rue); *omaneki* (very polite) – (oh-mah-nay-kee)
  I want to invite you to a nightclub.
  Naitokurabu ni shōtai shitai desu.
  (night-kuu-rah-buu nee show-tie she-tie dess)

invoice – *okurijō* (oh-kuu-ree-joe)
  What items must be included on the sales invoice?
  Shōgyō okurijō ni wa donna kōmoku wo kisai shimasu ka?
  (show-g'yoe oh-kuu-ree-joe nee wah doan-nah koe-moe-kuu oh kee-sigh she-mahss kah)

invoice, commercial – *shōgyō okurijō* (show-g'yoe oh-kuu-ree-joe)

invoice, consular – *ryōji shōmei okurijō* (rio-jee show-may oh-kuu-ree-joe)

invoice, pro forma – *mitsumori okurijō* (meet-sue-moe-ree oh-kuu-ree-joe)

issue (of a publication or stock) – *hakkō* (hock-koe)

issue; publish – *hakkō suru* (hock-koe sue-rue)

issue (stocks) – *hakkō zumi kabushiki* (hock-koe zuu-me kah-buu-she-kee)

italics (type style) – *itarikku tai* (ee-tah-ree-kuu tie)

item – *kōmoku* (koe-moe-kuu)

itemize – *meisaika suru* (may-sigh-kah sue-rue)

itemized account – *meisai seisansho* (may-sigh say-sahn-show)

— J —

jacket (book cover) – *kaba* (kah-bah)

Japan Agriculture and Forestry Standard (JAS) – *JASU* (jah-sue)

Japan Chamber of Commerce & Industry – *Nihon Shōkō Kaigisho* (nee-hone show-koe kye-ghee-show)

Japan Economic Journal – *Nihon Keizai Shinbun* (nee-hone kay-zye sheem-boon)

Japanese food – *Nihon shoku* (nee-hone show-kuu); *washoku* (wah-show-kuu)

This is the first time I've had Japanese food.
  Washoku wa hajimete desu.
    (wah-show-kuu wah hah-jee-may-tay dess)

Japanese language edition – *Nihongo no shinpan* (nee-hone-go no sheem-pahn)

Japanese style – *Nihonteki na* (nee-hone-tay-kee nah)

"Japanese telepathy" – *ishin denshin* (ee-sheen den-sheen)

Japan External Trade Organization (JETRO) – *Nihon Bōeki Shinkōkai* (nee-hone boe-ay-kee sheen-koe-kye)

Japan Industrial Standard (JIS) – *JISU* (jee-sue); *Nihon Kōgyō Kikaku* (nee-hone koe-g'yoe kee-kah-kuu)

Japan-oriented (toward Japan, for Japan) – *Nihon muke* (nee-hone-muu-kee)

jet lag – *jisa boke* (jee-sah boe-kay)

I'm really suffering from jet lag.
  Hidoku jisa boke wo shiteimasu.
    (he-doe-kuu jee-sah boe-kay oh shtay-mahss)

job/position – *shoku* (show-kuu); *shigoto* (she-go-toe)

job analysis – *shokumu bunseki* (show-kuu-muu boon-say-kee)

jobber (wholesaler) – *oroshiya* (oh-roe-she-yah)

job classification – *shokumu-kyū* (show-kuu-muu-cue)

job description – *shokumu kijutsu-sho* (show-kuu-muu kee-jute-sue-show)

job evaluation – *shokumu hyōtei* (show-kuu-muu h'yoe-tay)

job-hopper – *jōshū tenshoku sha* (joe-shuu ten-show-kuu shah)

job security – *shigoto no hoshō* (she-go-toe no hoe-show)

joint account – *kyōdō yokin kōza* (k'yoe-doe yoe-keen koe-zah)

   I have a joint account with my wife.

     Kannai to kyōdō yokin kōza wo motte imasu.

     (kah-nigh toe k'yoe-doe yoe-keen koe-zah oh moat-tay ee-mahss)

joint liability – *rentai sekinin* (ren-tie say-kee-neen)

joint owner – *kyōyū sha* (k'yoe-yuu shah)

joint stock company – *kabushiki gaisha* (kah-buu-she-kee guy-shah)

joint venture – *gōben* (go-ben)

joint venture company – *gōben gaisha* (go-ben guy-shah)

   I want to form a joint venture company.

     Gōben gaisha wo tsukuritai desu.

     (go-ben guy-shah oh t'sue-kuu-ree-tie dess)

judge (official) – *saibankan* (sigh-bahn-kahn)

judge, to – *handan suru* (hahn-dahn sue-rue)

judgement – *shinpan* (sheem-pahn)

junior (subordinate) – *kōhai* (koe-high)

   This is my junior. (usually used in reference to graduates of the same school)

Kono hito wa watakushi no kōhai desu.
(koe-no shtoe wah wah-tock-she no koe-high dess)
jurisdiction – *shihō ken* (she-hoe ken)
just (tight, close) – *giri giri* (ghee-ree ghee-ree)
justice – *seigi* (say-ghee)
justify (lines of type) – *gyō no sayū wo soroeru*
    (g'yoe no sah-yuu oh so-roe-ay-rue)

— K —

karaoke – *karaoke* (kah-rah-oh-kay)
  Let's go to a karaoke bar tonight.
  Konban karaoke bā ni ikimashō.
  (comb-bahn kah-rah-oh-kay bah nee ee-kee-mah-show)
keep one waiting – *mataseru* (mah-tah-say-rue)
  I'm sorry I kept you waiting.
  O-matase itashimashita.
  (oh-mah-tah-say ee-tah-she-mahsh-tah)
keyboard (computer) – *kii bōdo* (kee boe-doe)
key currency – *kijikutsūka* (kee-jee-kuu-t'sue-kah)
key man insurance – *jigyō-ka hoken* (jee-g'yoe-kah hoe-ken)
key industry – *kikan sangyō* (kee-kahn sahn-g'yoe)
  Are you buying key industry stocks?
  Kikan sangyō kabu wo katteimasu ka?
  (kee-kahn sahn-g'yoe kah-buu oh kah-tay-ee-mahss kah)
kickback – *ribēto* (ree-bay-toe)
kilogram – *kiro* (kee-roe)
kind (type) – *shurui* (shuu-rue-ee)
  How many types do you have?
  Nan shurui arimasu ka?
  (nahn shuu-rue-ee ah-ree-mahss kah)
kiting (checks) – *yūzū tegata no furidashi* (yuu-zuu tay-gah-tah no fuu-ree-dah-she)
knockdown (unassembled) – *kumitate-shiki* (kuu-me-tah-tay-she-kee)
  Can I buy this knocked-down?
  Kore wo kumitate-shiki de kaemasu ka?

    (koe-ray oh kuu-me-tah-tay she-kee day kye-mahss kah)

knockdown exports – *genchi kumitate yushutsu* (gen-chee kuu-me-tah-tay yuu-shoot-sue)

knockdown prices – *kumitate saitei kakaku* (kuu-me-tah-tay sigh-tay kah-kah-kuu)

knot (nautical mile) – *notto* (not-toe)

knowhow – *no hau* (no how)

knowledge – *chishiki* (chee-she-kee)

— L —

labor – *rōdō* (roe-doe)
laboratory – *kenkyūjo* (ken-cue-joe)
labor code – *rōdō kiyaku* (roe-doe kee-yah-kuu)
labor dispute – *rōdō sōgi* (roe-doe so-ghee)
laborer (worker) – *rōdō-sha* (roe-doe-shah)
labor force – *rōdō ryoku* (roe-doe rio-kuu)
labor-intensive industry – *rōdō shūyaku sangyō* (roe-doe shuu-yah-kuu sahn-g'yoe)
labor laws – *rōdō hō* (roe-doe hoe)
labor market – *rōdō shijō* (roe-doe she-joe)
labor relations – *rōshi kankei* (roe-she kahn-kay)
labor-saving – *rōdō setsuyaku-teki* (roe-doe say-t'sue-yah-kuu-tay-kee)
labor turnover – *rōdō idō* (roe-doe ee-doe)
labor union – *rōdō kumiai* (roe-doe kuu-me-eye)
labor union leaders – *rōdō kumiai kanbu* (roe-doe kuu-me-eye kahn-buu)
land – *tochi* (toe-chee)
landed cost – *rikuage hi komi nedan* (ree-kuu-ah-gay he koe-me nay-dahn)
landing certificate – *rikuage shōmei sho* (ree-kuu-ah-gay show-may show)
landing charges – *rikuage hi* (ree-kuu-ah-gay he)
land owner – *ji nushi* (jee nuu-she)
land tax – *chi so* (chee so)
large scale – *ōguchi* (oh-guu-chee)
largest – *saidai* (sigh-dye)
laser – *rēzā* (ray-zah)
laser beam printer – *rēzā biimu purinta* (ray-zah bee-muu puu-reen-tah)
laser processing – *rēzā kakō* (ray-zah kah-koe)

last ten days of the month – *gejun* (gay-june)

law – *hōki* (hoe-kee); *hōritsu* (hoe-ree-t'sue)

lawsuit – *soshō* (so-show)

lawyer – *bengoshi* (ben-go-she)
  Japanese companies usually do not use lawyers.
  Futsū Nihon no kaisha wa bengoshi wo tsukaimasen.
  (fuu-t'sue nee-hone no kye-shah wah ben-go-she oh sky-mah-sen)

layoff – *reiofu* (ray-oh-fuu); *ichiji kaiko* (ee-chee-jee kye-koe)

layout (for ad or page makeup) – *haichi* (high-chee)

leader – *shidō sha* (she-doe shah)

leadership – *shidō* (she-doe)

learn a lesson from (be instructive) – *benkyō ni naru* (ben-k'yoe nee nah-rue)

lease – *riisu* (ree-sue)

leave to (someone else) – *makaseru* (mah-kah-say-ruu)

lecture – *kōen* (koe-en)
  I'm going to a lecture tomorrow.
  Ashita kōen ni ikimasu.
  (ah-shtah koe-en nee ee-kee-mahss)

lecture hall (auditorium) – *kōdō* (koe-doe)

ledger – *moto-chō* (moe-toe-choe)

legal – *hōritsu-teki* (hoe-ree-t'sue-tay-kee)

legal advisor – *komon bengoshi* (koe-moan ben-go-she)

legal entity – *hō-teki jittai* (hoe-tay-kee jeet-tie)

legal holiday – *kōkyū bi* (koe-cue bee)
  The day after tomorrow is a legal holiday.
  Asatte wa kōkyū bi desu.
  (ah-sah-tay wah koe-cue bee dess)

legal monopoly – *hōtei dokusen* (hoe-tay doke-sen)

legislation (bill) – *an* (ahn)

lessee – *chingari-nin* (cheen-gah-ree-neen)

lesson – *keiko* (kay-koe)

lessor – *chingashi-nin* (cheen-gah-she-neen)

less than – *ika* (ee-kah)

letter – *tegami* (tah-gah-me)

letter of credit (LC) – *eru shii* (ay-rue she); *shin'yō jō* (sheen-yoe joe); letter-of-credit payable at sight – *eru shii ikkai barai* (ee-rue she-ee ee-kye bah-rye)

letter of indemnity – *nen sho* (nen show)

letter of introduction – *shōkai jō* (show-kye joe)
  I have a letter of introduction from Mr. Shimizu.
    Shimizu-san no shōkai jō wo motte imasu.
    (she-me-zuu-sahn no show-kye joe oh moat-tay ee-mahss)

letter of resignation – *jihyō* (jee-h'yoe)

liability – *saimu* (sigh-muu)

liability, actual – *jisshitsu saimu* (jeesh-sheet-sue sigh-muu)

liability, assumed – *keishō saimu* (kay-show sigh-muu)

liability, contingent – *gūhatsu saimu* (guu-hot-sue sigh-muu)

liability, current – *ryūdō fusai* (r'yuu-doe fuu-sigh)

liability, fixed – *kotei fusai* (koe-tay fuu-sigh)

liability insurance – *sekinin hoken* (say-kee-neen hoe-ken)

liability, secured – *tanpo tsuki fusai* (tahn-poe ski fuu-sigh)

liability, unsecured – *mu-tanpo fusai* (muu-tahn-poe fuu-sigh)

libel – *meiyo kison* (may-yoe kee-soan)

license – *menkyo* (men-k'yoe)
  Did you bring your license?
    Menkyo wo motte kimashita ka?
    (men-k'yoe oh moat-tay kee-mah-shtah kah)

license fees – *tokkyo ken shiyō ryō* (toke-yoe ken she-yoe rio)

licensing agreement – *raisensu keiyaku* (rye-sen-sue kay-yah-kuu)

lien – *sashiosae ken* (sah-she-oh-sigh ken)

life cycle (of product) – *seihin jumyō* (say-heen jume-yoe)

life insurance – *seimei hoken* (say-may hoe-ken)

life insurance policy – *seimei hoken shōken* (say-may hoe-ken show-ken)

lifetime – *shōgai* (show-guy)

lifetime employment – *shūshin koyō* (shuu-sheen koe-yoe)

lifetime of a patent – *tokkyo ken no sonzoku kikan* (toke-yoe ken-no soan-zoe-kuu kee-kahn)

light (weight) – *karui* (kah-rue-ee)

limit; limits – *kagiri* (kah-ghee-ree)

limited liability – *yūgen sekinin* (yuu-gen say-kee-neen)

limited partnership – *gōshi gaisha* (go-she guy-shah)

line (limit) – *sen* (sen)

line drawing – *sen ga* (sen gah)

line executive – *rain bumon kanbu shokuin* (rine buu-moan kahn-buu show-kuu-een)

line of management – *rain bumon kanri* (rine buu-moan kahn-ree)

line of business – *eigyō hinmoku* (ay-g'yoe heen-moe-kuu)

line of type – *gyō* (g'yoe)

line printer – *rain purinta* (rine print-ah)

liquid assets – *ryūdō shisan* (r'yuu-doe she-sahn)

liquidation – *seisan* (say-sahn)

liquidation value – *seisan kachi* (say-sahn kah-chee)

liquidity – *ryūdō sei* (r'yuu-doe say)

list (of names) – *meibo* (may-bow)

I will give you a list of names.
Meibo wo sashiagemasu.

(may-boe oh sah-she-ah-gay-mahss)
list (compile, write down) – *mokuroku ni kinyū suru*
(moe-kuu-roe-kuu nee keen-yuu sue-rue)
list (chart, timetable) – *hyō* (he-yoe)
listed securities – *jōjō shōken* (joe-joe show-ken)
list price – *hyōji kakaku* (h'yoe-jee kah-kah-kuu)
litigation – *soshō* (so-show)
We are now involved in litigation.
Ima soshō wo shiteimasu.
(ee-mah so-show oh shtay-mahss)
livelihood – *seikei* (say-kay)
loan – *shakkin* (shock-keen); *rōn* (roan); *kashi* (kah-she)
lobbyist – *robiisuto* (roe-bee-ee-stow); to lobby – *chinjō* (cheen-joe)
lobby of hotel – *robii* (roe-bee)
I'll meet you in the lobby.
Robii de aimashō.
(roe-bee day eye-mah-show)
local – *chihō no* (chee-hoe no)
local customs (tax authorities) – *chihō zeikan* (chee-hoe zay-kahn)
local hire (personnel hired locally) – *genchi saiyō* (gen-chee sigh-yoe)
local tax – *chihō zei* (chee-hoe zay)
logo – *rogo* (roe-go); *shinboru māku* (sheen-boe-rue mah-kuu)
long-range planning – *chōki keikaku* (choe-kee kay-kah-kuu)
long-term – *chōki no* (choe-kee no)
long-term debt – *chōki kari-ire kin* (choe-kee kah-ree-ee-ray keen)
loss – *sonshitsu* (soan-sheet-sue); *son wo suru* (soan oh sue-rue)
Last month I lost a lot of money.

Sengetsu takusan son wo shimashita.
(sen-gate-sue tock-sahn soan oh she-mah-shtah)

loss leader – *medama shōhin* (may-dah-mah show-heen)

lot (quite a bit) – *takusan* (tock-sahn)

low – *hikui* (he-kuu-ee)

lower yen quotation – *en yasu* (en yah-sue)

low income – *tei shotoku* (tay show-toe-kuu)

low interest loan – *tei kinri rōn* (tay keen-ree roan)

low-yield bonds – *tei rimawari saiken* (tay ree-mah-wah-ree sigh-ken)

loyalty – *chūgi* (chew-ghee); loyalty to one's self, company, country – *chūsei* (chew-say)

lump-sum – *sōgaku* (so-gah-kuu)

luxurious – *zeitaku* (zay-tah-kuu); *gōka* (go-kah)
Your home is really luxurious.
Anata no o-uchi wa hontō ni gōka desu.
(ah-nah-tah no oh-uu-chee wah hone-toe nee go-kah dess)

luxury goods – *zeitaku hin* (zay-tah-kuu heen)

luxury tax – *shashi zei* (shah-she zay)

— M —

machine – *kikai* (kee-kye)
machine tools – *kōsaku kikai* (koe-sah-kuu kee-kye)
magazine – *zasshi* (zahsh-she); monthly magazine –
gekkan shi (gay-kahn she)
  Do you take Fortune magazine?
  Fōchun zasshi wo totte imasu ka?
  (foe-chuun zah-she oh tote-tay ee-mahss kah)
magnet (natural) – *jitetsu* (je-tate-sue), instrument –
jishaku (jee-shah-kuu); *magunetto* (mah-guu-net-toe)
mailing list – *yūsō saki meibo* (yuu-so sah-kee may-
boe)
mail order – *mēru ōdā* (may-rue oh-dah); *tsūshin
hanbai* (t'sūe-sheen hahn-by)
main goal (purpose) – *konpon-teki na mokuteki* (cone-
poan-tay-kee nah moe-kuu-tay-kee)
main road (main highway) – *hōn dō* (hone doe)
maintenance – *iji* (ee-jee); *hoshu suru* (hoe-shuu sue-
rue)
maintenance contract – *hoshu keiyaku* (hoe-shuu
kay-yah-kuu)
majority interest – *kahansū kabushiki mochibun*
(kah-han-sue kah-buu-she-kee moe-chee-boon)
maker (manufacturer) – *mēka* (may-kah); *seisansha*
(say-sahn-shah)
manage – *keiei suru* (kay-ay sue-rue)
managed costs – *manējido kosuto* (mah-nay-jee-doe
cost-oh)
managed economy – *kanri keizai* (kahn-ree kay-zye)
management – *kanri* (kahn-ree); *keiei* (kay-ay)
management by objectives – *mokuhyō kanri* (moe-
kuu-h'yoe kahn-ree)

management chart – *kanri katsudō hyō* (kahn-ree cot-sue-doe h'yoe)

management consultant – *keiei konsarutanto* (kay-ay cone-sah-rue-tahn-toe)

management group – *manejimento gurūpu* (mah-nay-jee-men-toe guu-rue-puu)

manager – *keiei sha* (kay-ay shah); *shihainin* (she-high-neen)

man hours – *nobe jikan* (no-bay jee-kahn)

manner – *monogoshi* (moe-no-go-she)

manpower – *jinteki shigen* (jeen-tay-kee she-gen)

manual labor – *rōmu* (roe-muu)

manual workers – *nikutai rōdōsha* (nee-kuu-tie roe-doe-shah)

manufacture (produce) – *seizō* (say-zoe)

manufacture for trial – *shisaku suru* (she-sah-kuu sue-rue)

manufactured goods – *seihin* (say-heen); *bussan* (buu-sahn)

manufacturer – *seizō gyōsha* (say-zoe g'yoe-shah); *seisansha* (say-sahn-shah)

manufacturer's representative – *seizō gyōsha dairiten* (say-zoe g'yoe-shah dye-ree-ten)

manufacturing capacity – *seizō nōryoku* (say-zoe no-rio-kuu)

manufacturing control – *seizō kanri* (say-zoe kahn-ree)

manufacturing expense – *seizō hi* (say-zoe he)

manufacturing industry – *kōgyō* (koe-g'yoe)

marine cargo insurance – *kamotsu kaijō hoken* (kah-moat-sue kye-joe hoe-ken)

mark down – *nesage suru* (nay-sah-gay sue-rue)

market (marketplace) – *shijō* (she-joe)

market access – *shijō e no sekkin* (she-joe ay no sake-keen)

market appraisal – *shijō hyōka* (shc-joe h'yoe-kah)
market concentration – *shijō shūchū* (she-joe shuu-chew)
market forces – *shijō no jissei* (she-joe no jeece-say)
market forecast – *shijō mitōshi* (she-joe me-toe-she)
We are now preparing a market forecast.
Ima shijō mitōshi wo yōi shite imasu.
(ee-mah she-joe mee-toe-she oh yoe-ee shtay ee-mahss)
market index – *shijō shisū* (she-joe she-sue)
marketing – *mākketingu* (mah-kay-teen-guu); *ichiba chōsa* (ee-chee-bah choe-sah)
marketing budget – *shijō kaitaku hi* (she-joe kye-tah-kuu he)
marketing concept – *mākketingu konseputo* (mah-kay-ting-uu cone-sepp-toe)
marketing plan – *mākketingu keikaku* (mah-kay-ting-uu kay-kah-kuu)
marketing strategy – *mākkettingu senryaku* (mah-kay-ting-guu sen-r'yah-kuu)
market management – *shijō kanri* (she-joe kahn-ree)
market penetration – *shijō shintō* (she-joe sheen-toe)
market plan – *shijō keikaku* (she-joe kay-kah-kuu)
market position – *shikyō* (she-k'yoe)
market potential – *hanbai kanō ryō* (hahn-by kahn-no rio)
market price – *sōba* (so-bah); *shika* (she-kah)
market report – *shikyō hōkoku* (she-k'yoe hoe-koe-kuu)
market research – *shijō chōsa* (she-joe choe-sah)
First it is necessary to do market research.
Saisho ni shijō chōsa wo shinakereba narimasen.
(sigh-show nee she-joe choe-sah oh she-nah-kay-ray-bah nah-ree-mah-sen)
market saturation – *shijō hōwa* (she-joe hoe-wah)

market share – *shijō sen'yū ritsu* (she-joe sen-yuu ree-t'sue)

market survey – *shijō chōsa* (she-joe choe-sah)

market trends – *shijō dōkō* (she-joe doe-koe)

market value – *shijō kakaku* (she-joe kah-kah-kuu)

markup – *neage* (nay-ah-gay)

We will mark everything up in January.
   Ichigatsu ni zenbu neage shimasu.
   (ee-chee-got-sue nee zem-buu nay-ah-gay she-mahss)

marriage ties – *kei batsu* (kay bah-t'sue)

mass communications – *masukomi* (mah-sue-koe-me)

mass marketing – *tairyō mākketingu* (tie-rio mah-kay-teen-guu)

mass media – *masu media* (mah-sue may-dee-ah)

mass meeting (rally) – *taikai* (tie-kye)

mass production – *tairyō seisan* (tie-rio say-sahn)

master of ceremonies – *shikaisha* (she-kye-shah)

match (game, bout) – *shiai* (she-eye)

materials (data, information) – *shiryō* (she-rio)

materials, raw – *zairyō* (zye-rio)

Where do you buy your raw materials?
   Zairyō wa doko de kaimasu ka?
   (zye-rio wah doe-koe day kye-mahss kah)

maternity leave – *shussan kyūka* (shuu-sahn cue-kah)

maturity date – *shiharai kijitsu* (she-hah-rye kee-jee-t'sue)

mayor – *shichō* (she-choe)

I would like to meet the mayor.
   Shichō ni o-ai shitai desu.
   (she-choe nee oh-eye she-tie dess)

maximize – *saidaigen ni katsuyō suru* (sigh-dye-gen nee cot-sue-yoe sue-rue)

maximum – *saikō* (sigh-koe)

means (way) – *shudan* (shuu-dahn)

measure – *hakaru* (hah-kah-rue)

mediation – *chōtei* (choe-tay)

medium and small enterprises – *chū shō kigyō* (chew show kee-g'yoe)

meeting – *kaigō* (kye-go); *kaigi* (kye-ghee)

meeting of board of directors – *torishimari yaku kaigi* (toe-ree-she-mah-ree yah-kuu kye-ghee)

member firm (of group) – *kamei gaisha* (kah-may guy-shah)

memo – *memo* (may-moe)
  Please prepare a memo by tomorrow afternoon.
    Ashita no gogo made ni memo wo yōi shite kudasai. (ah-shtah no go-go mah-day nee may-moe oh yoe-ee shtay kuu-dah-sigh)

merchandise (goods) – *shōhin* (show-heen)

merge – *gappei suru* (gah-pay sue-rue)

merger – *kyūshū gappei* (cue-shuu gah-pay)

merit – *jitsuryoku* (jee-t'sue-rio-kuu); *kachi* (kah-chee)

merits and demerits – *tokushitsu* (toe-kuu-sheet-sue)

message – *okotozuke* (oh-koe-toe-zuu-kay); *messēji* (may-say-jee)

metals – *kinzoku* (keen-zoe-kuu)

method (way) – *hōhō* (hoe-hoe)

micro camera – *maikuro kamera* (my-kuu-roe kah-may-rah)

micro cassette recorder – *maikuro kasetto rekōda* (myu-kuu-roe kah-say-toe ray-koe-dah)

micro chip – *maikuro chippu* (my-kuu-roe cheap-puu)

microwave oven – *denshi renji* (den-she rain-jee)

mid-career recruitment – *chūto saiyō* (chew-toe sigh-yoe)

middle (between minimum and maximum) – *saichū* (sigh-chew)

middleman – *chūkan gyōsha* (chew-kahn g'yoe-shah)

middle management – *midoru manējimento* (me-doe-rue mah-nay-jee-men-toe); *bukachō* (buu-kah-choe)

middle of the month – *chūjun* (chew-june)

mile – *mairu* (my-rue)

mileage – *sōkō mairu sū* (so-koe my-rue sue)

millionaire – *hyakumanchōja* (h'yah-kuu-mahn-choe-jah)

mini computer – *mini konpyūta* (me-nee comb-pew-tah)

minimum – *saitei* (sigh-tay)

minimum charge – *saitei ryōkin* (sigh-tay rio-keen)
How much is the minimum charge?
> *Saitei ryōkin wa ikura desu ka?*
> (sigh-tay rio-keen wah ee-kuu-rah dess kah)

minimum wage – *saitei chingin* (sigh-tie cheen-gheen)

Ministry of Finance – *Ōkurashō* (oh-kuu-rah-show)

Ministry of International Trade & Industry (MITI) – *Tsūshō Sangyōshō* (t'sue-show sahn-g'yoe-show)

minority interest – *shōsū kabunushi mochibun* (show-sue kah-buu-nuu-she moe-chee-boon)

miscellaneous (items) – *zatta na* (zaht-tah nah)

miscellaneous expenses – *zappi* (zahp-pee)

miscellaneous goods – *zakka* (zahk-kah)

misunderstand – *gokai suru* (go-kye sue-rue)
I'm sorry, I misunderstood.
> *Sumimasen, gokai shimashita.*
> (sue-me-mah-sen go-kye she-mah-shtah)

There has been a misunderstanding.
> *Gokai ga arimashita.*
> (go-kye gah ah-ree-mah-shtah)

mobility of labor – *rōdō ryoku no idōsei* (roe-doe rio-kuu-no ee-doe-say)

mode – *mōdo* (moe-doe)

model (vehicle, etc) – *moderu* (moe-day-rue)

modem – *modemu* (moe-day-muu)

modern – *kindai-teki na* (keen-dye-tay-kee nah)

monetary base – *zaisei kiban* (zye-say kee-bahn)

monetary policy – *kin'yū seisaku* (keen-yuu say-sah-kuu)

money – *okane* (oh-kah-nay); *tsūka* (t'sue-kah)

money market – *kin'yū shijō* (keen-yuu she-joe)

money order – *yūbin gawase* (yuu-bean gah-wah-say

monitor – *monita* (moe-nee-tah)

monkey business (lie, cheat, unfair practices) – *inchiki* (een-chee-kee); illegitimate business – *inchiki shōbai* (een-chee-kee show-by)

monopoly – *dokusen* (doke-sen)

monthly payment – *geppu* (gape-puu)

monthly salary – *gekkyū* (gake-cue)

moonlighting – *fukugyō* (fuu-kuu-g'yoe)

morale – *kinrō iyoku* (keen-roe ee-yoe-kuu)

morality (ethics) – *dōtoku* (doe-toe-kuu)

moratorium (on payment) – *shiharai teishi* (she-hah-rye tay-she)

more than – *ijō* (eee-joe)

morning meeting – *chōrei* (choe-ray)

mortgage – *teitō ken* (tay-toe-ken)

mortgage bank – *tanpo gashi ginkō* (tahn-poe-gah-she gheen-koe)

mortgage bond – *tanpo tsuki saiken* (tahn-poe ski sigh-ken)

mortgage debenture – *tanpo tsuki shasai ken* (tahn-poe ski shah-sigh ken)

most-favored nation – *saikei koku* (sigh-kay koe-kuu)

motor – *mōta* (moe-tah)

motor drive (camera, etc.) – *mōtā doraibu* (moe-tah doe-rye-buu)

moving expenses – *hikkoshi hiyō* (heek-koe-she he-yoe)

Is your company going to pay moving expenses?
Kaisha ga hikkoshi hiyō wo haraimasu ka?
(kye-shah gah heek-koe-she he-yoe oh hah-rye-mahss kah)

multilateral agreement – *takoku kan kyōtei* (tah-koe-kuu kahn k'yoe-tay)

multilateral trade – *takaku bōeki* (tah-kah-kuu boe-ay-kee)

multinational corporation – *takokuseki kigyō* (tah-koe-kuu-say-kee kee-g'yoe)

multiple exchange rate – *fukusū kawase sōba* (fuu-kuu-sue kah-wah-say so-bah)

multiple taxation – *fuku zei* (fuu-kuu zay)

multi-unit apartment – *danchi* (dahn-chee)

mutual responsibility – *taigai no sekinin* (tie-guy no say-kee-neen)

mutual understanding – *sōgo no ryōkai* (so-go no rio-kye)

— N —

name (nominate, designate) – *shimei suru* (she-may
sue-rue)

name card – *meishi* (may-she)
  I would like to order some new name cards.
  Atarashii meishi wo chūmon shitai desu.
  (ah-tah-rah-she may-she oh chew-moan she-tie
  dess)

named inland point of (product) origin –
gensankoku nai shitei chiten (gen-sahn-koe-kuu nigh
she-tay chee-ten)

named point of destination – *shitei shimukai chiten*
(she-tay she-muu-kye chee-ten)

named point of exportation – *shitei yushutsu chiten*
(she-tay yuu-shoot-sue chee-ten)

named point of origin – *shitei gensan chiten* (she-tay
gen-sahn chee-ten)

named port of importation – *shitei yunyū kō* (she-
tay yuun-yuu koe)

name seal/stamp – *hanko* (hahn-koe); registered seal
used when signing official documents – *jitsu-in* (jee-
t'sue-een)
  May I use my name stamp?
  Hanko wo tsukatte mo ii desu ka?
  (hahn-koe oh t'sue-cot-tay moe ee dess kah)
  I don't have a name stamp. Will a signature do?
  Hanko wo motteimasen. Sain de ii desu ka?
  (hahn-koe oh moat-tay-mah-sen sign day ee dess
  kah)

national bank – *kokuritsu ginkō* (koe-kuu-ree-t'sue
gheen-koe)

national debt – *kokka saimu* (coke-kah sigh-muu)

National Diet – *Kokkai Gijidō* (coke-kye ghee-jee-doe)

nationalization – *kokuyūka* (koe-kuu-yuu-kah)

national tax – *koku zei* (koe-kuu zay)

National Tax Administration – *Koku Zei Cho* (koe-kuu zay choe)

nation-wide – *zenkoku* (zen-koe-kuu)
  We are doing business nation-wide.
    Zenkoku de torihiki wo shite imasu.
    (zen-koe-kuu day toe-ree-he-kee oh shtay ee-mahss)

natural resources – *tennen shigen* (ten-nen she-gen)

negative (film for printing) – *nega* (nay-gah)

negative cash flow – *genkin ryūshutsu* (gen-keen r'yuu-shoot-sue)

negotiable – *jōto dekiru* (joe-toe day-kee-rue)

negotiate – *kōshō suru* (koe-show sue-rue)

negotiated sale – *shōdan ni yoru hanbai* (show-dahn nee yoe-rue hahn-by)

negotiations – *kōshō* (koe-show); *shōdan* (show-dahn)
  We are now in the midst of negotiations.
    Ima kōshō chū desu.
    (ee-mah koe-show chew dess)

net assets – *jun shisan* (june she-sahn)

net cash flow – *netto kyasshu furō* (net-toe k'yah-shuu fuu-roe)

net income – *jun shotoku* (june show-toe-kuu); *tedori ni* (tay-doe-ree nee)

net investment – *jun tōshi* (june toe-she)

net profit – *jun eki* (june ay-kee)
  We will split the net profits fifty-fifty.
    Jun eki wa hanbun-hanbun ni wakemashō.
    (june ay-kee wah hahn-boon-hahn-boon nee wah-kay-mah-show)

net sales – *jun uriage daka* (june uu-ree-ah-gay dah-kah)

net worth – *shōmi shisan* (show-me she-sahn)

new model (type) – *shingatu* (sheen-gah-tah)

new product – *shin seihin* (sheen say-heen)

new product development – *shin seihin kaihatsu*
(sheen say-heen kye-hot-sue)

news – *nyūsu* (nuu-sue); *shirase* (she-rah-say)

newspaper – *shinbun* (sheem-boon)

Do you carry (stock) The New York Times?
Nū Yōku Taimuzu wo o-mochi desu ka?
(nuu-yoe-kuu time-zuu oh oh-moe-chee dess kah)

newsprint – *shinbun yō shi* (sheem-boon yoe she)

night club – *naito kurabu* (night-oh kuu-rah-buu)

night depository – *yakan yokin hokansho* (yah-kahn
yoe-keen hoe-kahn-show)

nondurable goods – *hi-taikyū zai* (he-tie-cue zye)

nonmember – *hi-kaiin* (he kye-een)

nonprofit company – *hi-eiri no kaisha* (he-ay-ree no
kye-shah)

nonresident – *hi-kyojūsha* (he-k'yoe-juu-shah)

nonvoting stock – *mugiketsuken kabushiki* (muu-
ghee-kate-sue-ken kah-buu-she-kee)

no par value – *mugakumen no* (muu-gah-kuu-men no)

notary public – *kōshō nin* (koe-show neen)

Can you introduce me to a good notary public?
Ii kōshō nin wo shōkai shite itadakemasu ka?
(ee koe-show neen oh show-kye shtay ee-tah-dah-
kee-mahss kah)

notary public office – *kōshō yakuba* (koe-show yah-
kuu-bah)

nuclear power – *genshi ryoku* (gen-she rio-kuu)

nuclear reactor – *genshi ro* (gen-she roe)

null and void – *mukō na* (muu-koe nah)

nullify (cancel) – *torikesu* (toe-ree-kay-sue)

Please cancel my order.
Chūmon wo torikeshite kudasai.
(chew-moan oh toe-ree-kay-shtay kuu-dah-sigh)

— O —

objections – *izon* (ee-zone)
  I have no objections.
    Izon wa arimasen.
    (ee-zone wah ah-ree-mah-sen)
objective (policy) – *hōshin* (hoe-sheen)
obligation (debt) – *saimu* (sigh-muu); duty – *gimu*
  (ghee-muu)
obsolescence – *chinpu* (cheen-puu)
obsolete – *fuyō no* (fuu-yoe no); *mō tsukawanai* (moe
  t'sue-kah-wah-nigh)
  That machine is obsolete.
    Sono kikai wa mō tsukaimasen.
    (so-no kee-kye wah moe t'sue-kye-mah-sen)
occupation – *shokugyō* (show-kuu-g'yoe)
  What is your occupation?
    Anata no go-shokugyō wa nan desu ka?
    (ah-nah-tah no go-show-kuu-g'yoe wah nahn dess
    kah)
occupational hazard – *shokugyō jō no kiken* (show-
  kuu'g-yoe joe no kee-ken)
occupation risk allowance – *kiken teate* (kee-ken
  tay-ah-tay)
odometer (automobile) – *sōkō kyori kei* (so-koe k'yoe-
  ree kay)
off duty – *hiban* (he-bahn)
offer – *teikyō suru* (tay-k'yoe sue-rue)
offer for sale – *uri ni dasu* (uu-ree nee dah-sue)
offered price – *yobi ne* (yoe-bee nay)
offered rate – *ofādo rēto* (oh-fah-doe ray-toe)
office – *ofisu* (oh-fee-sue); *jimusho* (jeem-show)
  What floor is your office on?

Ofisu wa nan kai desu ka?

(oh-fee-sue wah nahn kye dess kah)

office branch – *shiten* (she-ten)

office management – *jimu kanri* (jee-muu kahn-ree)

official (government representative) – *ōyake* (oh-yah-kay)

official/formal (wear, etc.) – *seishiki no* (say-she-kee no)

official business – *kōmu* (koe-muu)

official business trip – *shutchō* (shuu-choe)

Mr. Honda is away on a business trip.

Honda-san wa shutchō shiteimasu.

(hone-dah-sahn wah shuu-choe shtay-mahss)

official employment – *hon saiyō* (hone sigh-yoe)

off-line (computer) – *ofu rain* (oh-fuu rine)

off-season – *kisetsu hazure* (kee-say-t'sue hah-zoo-ray)

offset printing – *ofusetto insatsu* (oh-fuu-set-toe een-sah-t'sue)

offshore company – *ofushoa kanpanii* (oh-fuu-show-ah kahn-pah-nee)

okay – *daijōbu* (dye-joe-buu)

Is this schedule okay?

Kono yotei wa daijōbu desu ka?

(koe-no yoe-tay wah dye-joe-buu dess kah)

omit – *shōryaku suru* (show-r'yah-kuu sue-rue)

on account sales – *kakeuri de* (kah-kay-uu-ree day)

on consignment – *itaku hanbai de* (ee-tah-kuu hahn-by day)

on demand – *yōkyū barai de* (yoe-cue bah-rye day)

one hundred million – *ichi oku* (ee-chee oh-kuu)

one-thousand-yen note – *sen en satsu* (sen en sought-sue)

Would you please change this into one-thousand-yen notes?

Sen en satsu ni shite kuremasu ka?

    (sen en sah-t'sue nee shtay kuu-ray-mahss kah)

open (doors, office) – *hiraku* (he-rah-kuu)

on-the-job training – *shokuba kunren* (show-kuu-bah coon-ren)

open account – *ōpun kanjō* (oh-puun kahn-joe)

open-door policy – *monko kaihō seisaku* (moan-koe kye-hoe say-sah-kuu)

opening balance – *kishu zandaka* (kee-shuu zahn-dah-kah)

opening price – *yoritsuki nedan* (yoe-ree-t'sue-kee nay-dahn)

open market – *kōkai shijō* (koe-kye she-joe)

operating budget – *eigyō yosan* (ay-g'yoe yoe-sahn)
   Have you already settled on an operating budget?
     Eigyō yosan wo mō kimemashita ka?
     (ay-g'yoe yoe-sahn oh moe kee-may-mah-shtah kah)

operating expenses – *eigyō hi* (ay-g'yoe he)

operating income – *eigyō shūeki* (ay-g'yoe shuu-ay-kee)

operating profit – *eigyō rijun* (ay-g'yoe ree-june)

operations management – *gyōmu kanri* (g'yoe-muu kahn-ree)

operator – *operēta* (oh-pay-ray-tah)

opportunity – *kikai* (kee-kye)
   I think this is a wonderful opportunity.
     Kore wa subarashii kikai da to omoimasu.
     (koe-ray wah sue-bah-rah-she kee-kye dah toe oh-moe-ee-mahss)

oppose – *hantai suru* (hahn-tie sue-rue)

optical cable – *hikari kēburu* (he-kah-ree kay-buu-rue)

optical computer – *hikari konpyūta* (he-kah-ree comb-pew-tah)

optical disc – *hikari disuku* (he-kah-ree disk-uu)

optical fiber – *hikari faiba* (he-kah-ree fye-bah)

option – *opushon* (ope-shone)

optional (choice) – *sentaku jiyū no* (sen-tah-kuu jee-yuu no)

optional equipment (for auto) – *opushon buhin* (ope-shone buu-heen)

oral bid – *kōtō nyūsatsu* (koe-toe nuu-sah-t'sue)

order (for merchandise/goods) – *chūmon suru* (chew-moan sue-rue); *hatchū suru* (hot-chew sue-rue)

order form – *chūmon shoshiki* (chew-moan show-she-kee)

Please bring me an order form.

Chūmon shoshiki wo motte kite kudasai.

(chew-moan show-she-kee oh moat-tay kee-tay kuu-dah-sigh)

order number – *chūmon bangō* (chew-moan bahn-go)

ordinary – *futsū* (fuu-t'sue)

ordinary deposit – *futsū yokin* (fuu-t'sue yoe-keen)

organization – *soshiki* (so-she-kee)

organization chart – *kaisha kikōzu* (kye-shah kee-koe-zuu)

organize (form) – *soshiki suru* (so-she-kee sue-rue)

original (copy) – *genbun* (gen-boon)

original (work) – *gensho* (gen-show)

original cost – *shutoku genka* (shuu-toe-kuu gen-kah)

out of order – *koshō* (koe-show)

out-of-pocket expenses – *keihi no ichiji tatekae* (kay-he no ee-chee-jee tah-tay-kye)

outlay – *shishutsu* (she-shoot-sue)

outlet – *hanro* (hahn-roe)

outline – *aramashi* (ah-rah-mah-she)

outlook – *mitōshi* (me-toe-she)

outside pressure – *gai-atsu* (guy-ah-t'sue)

outstanding debt – *miharai saimu* (me-hah-rye sigh-muu)

outstanding stock – *shagai kabu* (shah-guy kah-buu)

overage – *kyōkyū kajō* (k'yoe-cue kah-joe)

overbuy – *kaisugiru* (kye-sue-ghee-rue)

overcharge – *hōgai na daikin seikyū* (hoe-guy nah dye-keen say-cue)

overdraft – *tōza kashikoshi* (toe-zah kah-she-koe-she)

overdue (payment) – *shiharai kigen ga sugita* (she-hah-rye kee-gen gah sue-ghee-tah)

overhead – *shogakari komi no* (show-gah-kah-ree koe-me no)

overpaid – *haraisugi no* (hah-rye-sue-ghee no)

over production — *seisan kajō* (say-sahn kah-joe)

overseas (in a foreign country) – *kaigai* (kye-guy); foreign location – *gaichi* (guy-chee)

overseas phone call – *kokusai denwa* (coke-sigh den-wah)

    Can I make an overseas phone call from this telephone?

        Kono denwa de kokusai denwa dekimasu ka?
        (koe-no dane-wah day koe-kuu-sigh dane-wah day-kee-mahss kah)

    Mr. Sato, you have an overseas phone call.
    Sato-san, kokusai denwa desu.
    (sah-toe-sahn coke-sigh den-wah dess)

oversell – *urisugiru* (uu-ree-sue-ghee-rue)

overstock – *zaiko kajō* (zye-koe kah-joe)

oversubscribed – *mōshikomi chōka no* (moe-she-koe-me choe-kah no)

oversupply – *kyōkyū kajō* (k'yoe-cue kah-joe)

over-the-counter quotation – *tentō torihiki sōba* (ten-toe toe-ree-he-kee so-bah)

overtime – *chōka kinmu* (choe-kah keen-muu)

overtime allowance – *chōka kinmu teate* (choe-kah keen-muu tay-ah-tay)

overvalued – *kadai hyōka sareta* (kah-dye h'yoe-kah sah-ray-tah)

overwork – *hatarakisugi* (hah-tah-rah-kee-sue-ghee)
owner – *shoyūsha* (show-yuu-shah); *mochinushi* (moe-chee-nuu-she)

Who is the owner of that shop?
Sono mise no mochinushi wa donata desu ka?
(so-no me-say no moe-che-nuu-she wah doe-nah-tah dess kah)

owner's equity – *shoyūsha mochibun* (show-yuu-shah moe-chee-boon)
ownership – *shoyūken* (show-yuu-ken)

— P —

pack (bags) – *nizukuri suru* (nee-zuu-kuu-ree sue-rue)
  Hurry! Pack your bags!
  Isoide! Nimotsu wo nizukuri shite!
  (ee-soy-day nee-moat-sue oh nee-zuu-kuu-ree shtay)
package (parcel) – *kozutsumi* (koe-zute-sue-me)
  Does this package belong to you?
  Kono kozutsumi wa anata no desu ka?
  (koe-no koe-zute-sue-me wah ah-nah-tah no dess kah)
  I want to mail this package.
  Kono kozutsumi wo yūbin de okuritai desu.
  (koe-no koe-zute-sue-me oh yuu-bean day oh-kuu-ree-tie dess)
package deal – *ikkatsu torihiki* (eek-cot-sue toe-ree-he-kee)
packaging – *hōsō* (hoe-so)
packing case – *yusō-yō hōsō bako* (yuu-so-yoe hoe-so bah-koe)
packing list – *hōsō meisaisho* (hoe-so may-sigh-show)
  Let me see the packing list.
  Hōsō meisaisho wo misete kudasai.
  (hoe-so may-sigh-show oh me-say-tay kuu-dah-sigh)
page – *pēji* (pay-jee)
paid holiday – *yūkyū kyūka* (you-cue cue-kah)
paid in full – *zengaku shiharaizumi* (zen-gah-kuu she-hah-rye-zuu-me)
paid-in surplus – *haraikomi jōyokin* (hah-rye-koe-me joe-yoe-keen)
paid-up capital – *haraikomizumi shihonkin* (hah-rye-koe-me-zuu-me she-hone-keen)

paid-up shares – *haraikomizumi kabu* (hah-rye-koo-me-zuu-me kah-buu)

pallet – *paretto* (pah-rate-toe)

palletized freight – *paretto yusō* (pah-rate-toe yuu-so)

pamphlet – *panfuretto* (pahn-fuu-rate-toe)

paper – *kami* (kah-me)

paperback (book) – *pēpābakku* (pay-pah-back-kuu)

par – *heika* (hay-kah)

par, above – *gakumen ijō no kakaku* (gah-kuu-men ee-joe no kah-kah-kuu)

par, below – *gakumen ika no kakaku* (gah-kuu-men ee-kah no kah-kah-kuu)

parcel post – *kozutsumi yūbin* (koe-zute-sue-me yuu-bean)

I will send it to you by parcel post.
   Kozutsumi de okurimasu.
   (koe-zute-sue-me day oh-kuu-ree-mahss)

parent company – *oya gaisha* (oh-yah guy-shah)

parity – *tōka* (toe-kah)

part (portion) – *ichibu* (ee-chee-buu)

partial payment – *bunkatsu haraikomi* (boon-cot-sue hah-rye-koe-me); *uchibarai* (uu-chee-bah-rye)

Will partial payment be all right?
   Uchibarai de yoroshii desu ka?
   (uu-chee-bah-rye day yoe-roe-she dess kah)

participation – *sanka* (sahn-kah)

participation fee – *sanka ryō* (sahn-kah rio)

participation loan – *kyōdō yūshi* (k'yoe-doe yuu-she)

partner (business) – *pātona* (pah-toe-nah); other party – *aite* (eye-tay)

partnership (company) – *gōmei gaisha* (go-may guy-shah)

parts (of products) – *buhin* (buu-heen)

part-time work – *arubaito* (ah-rue-by-toe)

Are you doing part-time work?

Arubaito wo shiteimasu ka?
(ah-rue-by-toe oh shtay-mahss kah)

party (Japanese style) – *enkai* (en-kye)

par value – *gakumen kakaku* (gah-kuu-men kah-kah-kuu)

passbook (bank) – *yokin tsūchō* (yoe-keen t'sue-choe)

passport control – *shukkoku tetsuzuki* (shuke-koe-kuu tay-t'sue-zuu-kee)

past due – *shiharai kigen keika* (she-hah-rye kee-gen kay-kah)

patent – *tokkyo* (toke-k'yoe)
Is this patented?
   Tokkyo wo totte arimasu ka?
   (toke-k'yoe oh tote-tay ah-ree-mahss kah)

patent application – *tokkyo ken shinsei* (toke-k'yoe ken sheen-say)

patented process – *tokkyo ken wo motsu seisan hōhō* (toke-k'yoe ken oh moat-sue say-sahn hoe-hoe)

patent law – *tokkyo hō* (toke-k'yoe hoe)

patent pending – *tokkyo shutsugan chū* (toke-k'yoe shuu-t'sue-gahn chew)

patent royalty – *tokkyo ken shiyō ryō* (toke-k'yoe ken she-yoe rio)

paternalism – *onjōshugi* (own-joe-shuu-ghee)

patience (perseverance) – *shinbō* (sheen-boe); patience (forbearance) – *gaman* (gah-mahn)
Please be patient.
   Shinbō shite kudasai.
   (sheen-boe shtay kuu-dah-sigh)

pattern (design) – *moyō* (moe-yoe)

pattern recognition (electronically) – *patān ninshiki* (pah-tahn neen-she-kee)

pay – *shiharau* (she-hah-rah-uu)

pay (wages) – *kyūryō* (cue-rio)

payable on demand – *yōkyū barai* (yoe-cue bah-rye)

payable to bearer – *jisan nin barai* (jee-sahn neen bah-rye)

pay-as-you-go system – *genkin-barai shugi* (gen-keen-bah-rye shuu-ghee)

payback period – *kaishū kikan* (kye-shuu kee-kahn)

payee – *uketori nin* (uu-kay-toe-ree neen)

payer – *shiharai nin* (she-hah-rye neen)

pay in full – *zengaku shiharai* (zen-gah-kuu she-hah-rye)

paymaster – *kaikei buchō* (kye-kay buu-choe)

payment – *shiharai* (she-hah-rye); *shikyū* (she-cue)
   When will payment be made?
   Shiharai wa itsu nasaimasu ka?
   (she-hah-rye wah eat-sue nah-sigh-mahss kah)

payment in full – *zengaku shiharai* (zen-gah-kuu she-hah-rye)

payment in kind – *genbutsu barai* (gen-boot-sue bah-rye)

payment of taxes – *nō zei* (no zay)

payoff (illegal action) – *zōwai* (zoe-why)

payout period – *kaishū kikan* (kye-shuu kee-kahn)

payroll – *kyūryō shiharai bo* (cue-rio she-hah-rye boe)

payroll tax – *kyūyo zei* (cue-yoe zay)

peak load – *piiku rōdo* (pee-kuu roe-doe)

pegged price – *kugizuke kakaku* (kuu-ghee-zuu-kay kah-kah-kuu)

penalty – *bakkin* (bahk-keen)

penalty clause – *iyaku jōkō* (ee-yah-kuu joe-koe)

pension (company) – *kōsei nenkin* (koe-say nen-keen); national (gov't) pension – *kokumin nenkin* (koe-kuu-mean nen-keen)

pension fund – *nenkin kikin* (nen-keen kee-keen)

pension system – *nenkin seido* (nen-keen say-doe)

per – *atari* (ah-tah-ree)

per capita – *hitori atari no* (shtoe-ree ah-tah-ree no)

percent – *pāsento* (pah-sen-toe)
How about a ten percent discount?
> *Juppāsento no waribiki wa dō desu ka?*
> (joop-pah-sen-toe no wah-ree-bee-kee wah doe dess kah)

percentage earnings – *buai shūnyū* (buu-eye shuun-yuu)

percentage of profits – *rieki ritsu* (ree-ay-kee ree-t'sue)

per diem – *ryohi nittō* (rio-he neat-toe)

perfect (complete) – *kanzen* (kahn-zen); *kanpeki* (kahn-pay-kee)

period (term) – *kikan* (kee-kahn)

periodic checkup – *teiki kensa* (tay-kee ken-sah)

periodic inventory – *teiki tanaoroshi* (tay-kee tah-nah-oh-roe-she)

peripheral equipment – *shūhen kiki* (shu-hen kee-kee)

per piece – *ikko ni tsuite* (eek-koe nee t'sue-ee-tay)

perks – *rinji teate* (reen-jee tay-ah-tay)

permanent – *kōkyū* (coke-yuu)

permit (permission) – *kyoka* (k'yoe-kah)
A permit is necessary.
> *Kyoka ga hitsuyō desu.*
> (k'yoe-kah gah heat-sue-yoe dess)

perpetual inventory – *keizoku tanaoroshi* (kay-zoe-kuu tah-nah-oh-roe-she)

per piece – *ikko ni tsuite* (eek-koe nee t'sue-ee-tay)

per share – *hitokabu atari no* (shtoe-kah-buu ah-tah-ree-no)

personal computer – *pasokon* (pah-so-cone)

personal connections – *kone* (koe-nay)
In Japan personal connections are especially important.
> *Nihon de kone wa toku ni jūyō desu.*

(nee-hone day koe-nay wah toe-kuu nee juu-yoe
dess)

personal history record (biographical resume) –
rireki sho (ree-ray-kee show)

I have not had time to read your personal history.
Rireki sho wo yomu jikan ga arimasen deshita.
(ree-ray-kee show oh yoe-muu jee-kahn gah ah-ree-
mah-sen desh-tah)

personal income tax – *kojin shotoku zei* (koe-jeen
show-toe-kuu zay)

personality – *seikaku* (say-kah-kuu); *jinkaku* (jean-
kah-kuu); *hitogara* (shtoe-gah-rah)

personal liability – *kojin songai baishō sekinin* (koe-
jeen soan-guy by-show say-kee-neen)

personal property – *dōsan* (doe-sahn)

person in charge – *tantō sha* (tahn-toe-shah); *kakari*
(kah-kah-ree)

Who is the person in charge?
Tantō sha wa donata deshō ka?
(tahn-toe shah wah doe-nah-tah day-show-kah)

person concerned – *hon nin* (hone neen)

The person concerned is not here today.
Hon nin wa kyō imasen.
(hone neen wah k'yoe ee-mah-sen)

personnel – *jin'in* (jeen-een)

personnel administration – *jinji kanri* (jeen-jee
kahn-ree)

personnel affairs – *jinji* (jeen-jee)

personnel department – *jinji bu* (jeen-jee buu)

personnel expense – *jinken hi* (jeen-ken he)

person-to-person – *shimei-tsūwa* (she-may-t'sue-wah)

pharmacist – *yakuzai-shi* (yah-kuu-zye-she)

pharmacy – *yakkyoku* (yahk-k'yoe-kuu)

phase in – *dankai-teki ni kumiireru* (dahn-kye tay-kee
nee kuu-me-ee-ray-rue)

phase out – *dankai-teki ni torinozoku* (dahn-kye tay-kee nee toe-ree-no-zoe-kuu)

phone – *denwa* (den-wah); return phone call – *ori-kaeshi denwa* (oh-ree-kye-she den-wah); call back – *kōru bakku* (koe-rue bah-kuu)

phone answering machine – *rusuban denwa* (rue-sue-bahn den-wah)

photographer – *kameraman* (kah-may-rah-mahn)

physical inventory – *jitchi tanaoroshi* (jee-chee tah-nah-oh-roe-she)

physician – *isha* (ee-shah)

pickup (meet at airport or station) – *mukae ni iku* (muu-kye nee ee-kuu)

    I will meet you (pick you up) at the airport.
    Kūkō ni o-mukae ni mairimasu.
    (kuu-koe nee oh-muu-kye nee my-ree-mahss)

pickup and delivery – *shūhai sābisu* (shuu-high sah-bee-sue)

piecework – *chin shigoto* (cheen she-go-toe)

pie chart – *en gurafu* (en guu-rah-fuu)

piggyback service – *pigii bakku sābisu* (pee-ghee bahk-kuu sah-bee-sue)

pilferage – *nukini* (nuu-kee-nee)

pill (medicinal) – *jōzai* (joe-zye)

place an order – *hatchū suru* (hot-chew sue-rue); (in a restaurant) – *chūmon suru* (chew-moan sue-rue)

place of business – *eigyō sho* (ay-g'yoe show)

place of work – *shokuba* (show-kuu-bah)

plan (planning, project) – *keikaku* (kay-kah-kuu)

planned obsolescence – *keikaku-teki rōkyū ka* (kay-kah-kuu tay-kee roe-cue kah)

planning department – *kikaku bu* (kee-kah-kuu buu)

plant capacity – *kōjō seisan nōryoku* (koe-joe say-sahn no-rio-kuu)

plant location – *kōjō no ichi* (koe-joe no ee-chee)

plant manager – *kōjō chō* (koe-joe choe)
plot of land (lot) – *tochi* (toe-chee)
pocket TV – *poketto terebi* (poe-ket-toe tay-ray-bee)
point of sale – *hanbai jiten* (hahn-by jee-ten)
polar coordinates robot – *kyoku zahyō robotto* (k'yoe-kuu zah-h'yoe roe-boat-toe)
policy – *seisaku* (say-sah-kuu); *hōshin* (hoe-sheen)
policy (insurance) – *hoken shōken* (hoe-ken show-ken)
policyholder – *hoken keiyaku sha* (hoe-ken kay-yah-kuu shah)
polite, be – *go-enryo suru* (go-en-rio sue-rue)
politicians – *seijika* (say-jee-kah)
politics – *seiji* (say-jee)
pollution – *kōgai* (koe-guy)
popular – *ryūkō* (ree-you-koe); *ninki ga aru* (neen-kee gah ah-rue)
population – *jinkō* (jeen-koe)
portable TV – *pōtaburu terebi* (poe-tah-buu-rue tay-ray-bee)
position (place) – *ichi* (ee-chee)
position (job) hunt – *kyūshoku suru* (cue-show-kuu sue-rue)
    I am seeking a job.
        Kyūshoku shite imasu.
        (cue-show-kuu shtay ee-mahss)
position seeker's guide – *kyūshoku annai* (cue-show-kuu ahn-nigh)
positive – *sekkyoku* (say-k'yoe-kuu)
positive (film) – *yōga* (yoe-gah); *poji* (poe-jee)
positive cash flow – *genkin ryūnyū* (gen-keen r'yuu-n'yuu)
possibility – *kanōsei* (kah-no-say)
    Is there any possibility (it will happen, etc)?
        Kanōsei ga arimasu ka?
        (kah-no-say gah ah-ree-mahss kah)

postage (cost) – *yūbin-dai* (yuu-bean-dye)

postal money order – *yūbin kawase* (yuu-bean kah-wah-say)

postdated – *jigo hizuke no* (jee-go he-zuu-kay no)

postpone – *enki suru* (en-kee sue-rue)

potential buyer – *mikomi kyaku* (me-koe-me k'yah-kuu)

potential sales – *hanbai kanōsei* (hahn-by kah-no-say)

power of attorney – *inin ken* (ee-neen ken)

Do you have power of attorney?

Inin ken wo motteimasu ka?

(ee-neen ken oh moe-tay-mahss kah)

power steering (vehicle) – *pawā sutearingu* (pah-wah sue-tay-ah-reen-guu)

practical – *jissai teki* (jeece-sigh tay-kee); *jitsuyō-teki na* (jee-t'sue-yoe tay-kee nah)

precision machinery – *seimitsu kikai* (say-meet-sue kee-kye)

prediction – *yogen* (yoe-gen)

preface (in book, etc) – *maegaki* (my-gah-kee)

prefectural governor – *chiji* (chee-jee)

prefecture – *ken* (ken)

preferred stock – *yūsen kabu* (yuu-sen kah-buu)

preferred tariff – *tokkei kanzei* (toke-kay kahn-zay)

preliminary prospectus – *kari shui sho* (kah-ree shuu-ee show)

premium payment – *hoken ryō haraikomi* (hoe-ken rio hah-rye-koe-me)

prepay – *maebarai suru* (my-bah-rye sue-rue)

prescription (medical) – *shohō-sen* (show-hoe-sen)

presentation – *kōen* (koe-en)

present condition – *genjō* (gen-joe)

president (of a company) – *shachō* (shah-choe)

What is the president's name?

Shachō no o-namae wa nan desu ka?

(shah-choe no oh-nah-my wah nahn dess kah)

preventive maintenance – *yobō hozen* (yoe-boe hoe-zen)

price (put price on) – *nedan wo tsukeru* (nay-dahn oh t'sue-kay-rue)

price (value) – *kakaku* (kah-kah-kuu); *nedan* (nay-dahn); original price – *moto ne* (moe-toe nay)

price cutting – *nesage* (nay-sah-gay)

price differential – *kakaku kakusa* (kah-kah-kuu kah-kuu-sah)

price-earnings ratio – *kabuka shūeki ritsu* (kah-buu-kah shuu-ay-kee ree-t'sue)

price increase – *neage* (nay-ah-gay)

price index – *bukka shisū* (buuk-kah she-sue)

price limit – *sashine* (sah-she-nay)

price list – *kakaku hyō* (kah-kah-kuu h'yoe)

Let me see the price list.

Kakaku hyō wo misete kudasai.

(kah-kah-kuu h'yoe wo me-say-tay kuu-dah-sigh)

price of goods – *bukka* (buu-kah)

price range – *kakaku tai* (kah-kah-kuu tie)

price support – *kakaku shiji* (kah-kah-kuu she-jee)

price war – *nesage kyōsō* (nay-sah-gay k'yoe-so)

pride – *hokori* (hoe-koe-ree)

He is a man of great pride.

Ano hito wa hokori no takai hito desu.

(ah-no shtoe wah hoe-koe-ree no tah-kye shtoe dess)

primary market – *shuyō shijō* (shuu-yoe she-joe)

primary reserves – *dai ichi shiharai junbi kin* (dye-ee-chee she-hah-rye juum-bee-keen)

prime rate – *puraimu rēto* (puu-rye-muu ray-toe)

prime time – *sai kōchō ki* (sigh koe-choe kee)

principal (key individual) – *hon nin* (hone neen)

principle – *gensoku* (gen-so-kuu); *shugi* (shuu-ghee)

print – *insatsu suru* (een-sah-t'sue sue-rue)

printed matter – *insatsu butsu* (een-sah-t'sue boot-sue)

Please send (mail) this as printed matter.

Kore wo insatsu butsu de okutte kudasai.

(koe-ray oh een-sah-t'sue boot-sue day oh-coot-tay kuu-dah-sigh)

printer – *insatsuya* (een-sah-t'sue-yah); *purinta* (puu-reen-tah)

printout (computer) – *purinto auto* (puu-reen-toe out-oh)

print-run (number of copies) – *shuppan bussū* (shuup-pahn buuse-sue)

priority – *yūsen ken* (yuu-sen ken)

private – *kojin* (koe-jeen)

Let's take a privately owned taxi.

Kojin takushii ni norimashō.

(koe-jeen tahk-she nee no-ree-mah-show)

private label – *jika shōhyō* (jee-kah show-h'yoe)

private matter – *shiteki na koto* (she-tay-kee nah koe-toe)

private placement of stock – *shibo* (she-boe)

private secretary – *hisho yaku* (he-show yah-kuu)

privilege – *tokuten* (toe-kuu-ten)

prize – *shōhin* (show-heen)

problem (question) – *mondai* (moan-dye)

Is there some problem?

Mondai ga arimasu ka?

(moan-dye gah ah-ree-mahss-kah)

problem analysis – *mondai bunseki* (moan-dye boon-say-kee)

problem occurs – *mondai ga okiru* (moan-dye gah oh-kee-rue)

problem solving – *mondai kaiketsu* (moan-dye kye-kate-sue)

procedure – *tetsuzuki* (tay-t'sue-zuu-kee)
  What is the proper procedure?
    Tadashii tetsuzuki wa nan deshō ka?
    (tah-dah-she tay-t'sue-zuu-kee wah nahn day-show kah)

process (v.) – *shori suru* (show-ree sue-rue)

procurement – *chōtatsu* (choe-tot-sue)

product – *seihin* (say-heen)

product analysis – *seihin bunseki* (say-heen boon-say-kee)

product design – *seihin sekkei* (say-heen sake-kay)

product development – *seihin kaihatsu* (say-heen kye-hot-sue)

product group – *seihin gurūpu* (say-heen guu-ruu-puu)

production – *seisan* (say-sahn); *seisandaka* (say-sahn-dah-kah)

production control – *seisan kanri* (say-sahn kahn-ree)
  Who is responsible for production control?
    Seisan kanri no sekinin sha wa donata desu ka?
    (say-sahn kahn-ree no say-kee-neen shah wah doe-nah-tah dess kah)

production costs – *seisan hi* (say-sahn he)

production line – *nagare sagyō* (nah-gah-ray sah-g'yoe)

production process – *seisan kōtei* (say-sahn koe-tay)

production schedule – *seizō yotei hyō* (say-zoe yoe-tay h'yoe)

productivity – *seisan sei* (say-sahn-say)

product life – *seihin jumyō* (say-heen juum-yoe)

product line – *seihin shumoku* (say-heen shuu-moe-kuu)

product management – *seihin kanri* (say-heen kahn-ree)

profession – *senmon shoku* (sen-moan-show-kuu)

profit – *rijun* (ree-june); *mōke* (moe-kay); *shūeki* (shuu-ay-kee); *rieki* (ree-ay-kee)

profitability – *shūeki sei* (shuu-ay-kee say)

profitability analysis – *shūeki ritsu bunseki* (shuu-ay-kee ree-t'sue boon-say-kee)

profitable – *yūri na* (yuu-ree nah)

profit-and-loss statement – *son-eki keisan sho* (soan-ay-kee kay-sahn show)

profit forecast – *rieki yosoku* (ree-ay-kee yoe-so-kuu)

profitless – *rieki no nai* (ree-ay-kee no nigh)

profit margin – *rizaya* (ree-zah-yah)

profit point – *saisan bēsu* (sigh-sahn bay-sue)

profit sharing – *rijun bunpai* (ree-june boon-pie)

profit taking – *rigui* (ree-gooey)

pro forma invoice – *mitsumori okurijō* (meet-sue-more-ree oh-kuu-ree-joe)

Please send a pro forma invoice.

Mitsumori okurijō wo okutte kudasai.

(meet-sue-moe-ree oh-kuu-ree-joe oh oh-kuu-tay kuu-dah-sigh)

pro forma statement – *mitsumori sho* (meet-sue-moe-ree show)

program (plan) – *keikaku* (kay-kah-kuu)

program, computer – *puroguramu* (puu-roe-guu-rah-muu)

progress – *shinpo* (sheem-poe); make progress – *shinpo suru* (sheem-poe sue-rue); *jōtatsu suru* (joe-tot-sue sue-rue); go ahead, go forward – *susumu* (sue-sue-muu)

prohibited – *kinshi* (keen-she)

prohibited goods – *kinsei hin* (keen-say heen)

project – *kikaku* (kee-kah-kuu); *jigyō* (jee-g'yoe)

Are you working on a new project now?

Ima atarashii kikaku wo yatte imasu ka?

(ee-mah ah-tah-rah-she kee-kah-ku oh yaht-tay ee-mahss kah)

projector – *eisha-ki* (ay-shah-kee)

project proposal in writing – *ringi sho* (reen-ghee show)

promise (appointment) – *yakusoku* (yah-kuu-so-kuu)

promissory note – *yakusoku tegata* (yah-kuu-so-kuu tay-gah-tah)

promote (to higher position/rank) – *shōshin saseru* (show-sheen sah-say-rue)

Congratulations on your promotion.

　　Go-shōshin omedetō gozaimasu.

　　(go-show-sheen oh-may-day-toe go-zye-mahss)

promotion for sales – *hanbai sokushin* (hahn-by so-kuu-sheen); *shinkō* (sheen-koe)

prompt answer – *sokutō* (so-kuu-toe)

prompt decision – *sokudan* (so-kuu-dahn)

proof – *kakushō* (kah-kuu-show); *shōko* (show-koe)

proof of loss – *songai shōmei sho* (soan-guy show-may-show)

proofread – *kōsei suru* (koe-say sue-rue)

proofreading – *kōsei* (koe-say)

property – *zaisan* (zye-sahn)

proposal (proposition) – *teian* (tay-ahn); *mōshikomi* (moe-she-koe-me)

proprietary – *shoyū nushi no* (show-yuu nuu-she no)

proprietary rights – *shoyū ken* (show-yuu ken)

proprietor – *shoyū sha* (show-yuu shah)

prospect (outlook) – *mitōshi* (me-toe-she)

prospective client – *mikomi kyaku* (me-koe-me k'yack-uu)

prospectus – *shui sho* (shuu-ee show); *kisoku sho* (kee-so-kuu show)

May I see your prospectus?

　　Shui sho wo mite mo yoroshii desu ka?

(shuu-ee show oh meet-ay moe yoe-roe-she dess
kah)

prosperity – *han'ei* (hahn-ay); to thrive – *ryūsei na*
(r'yuu-say nah)

protectionism – *hogo bōeki shugi* (hoe-go boe-ay-kee
shuu-ghee)

protective tariff – *hogo kanzei* (hoe-go kahn-zay)

provocative – *shigeki-teki* (she-gay-kee-tay-kee)

prove (verify) – *shōmei suru* (show-may sue-rue)

proxy – *dairi* (dye-ree)

proxy statement – *inin jō* (ee-neen joe)

public – *ōyake* (oh-yah-kay)

public auction – *kyōbai* (k'yoe-by)

public domain (patent) – *kenri shōmetsu jōtai* (ken-
ree show-mate-sue joe-tie)

public funds – *kōkin* (koe-keen)

publicity – *senden* (sen-den)

public offering – *kōbo* (koe-boe)

public opinion poll – *yoron chōsa* (yoe-roan choe-sah)

public property – *kōyū zaisan* (koe-yuu zye-sahn)

public relations – *shōgai* (show-guy); PR – *pii-āru*
(pee-ah-rue)

public relations department – *shōgai bu* (show-buy
buu); *PR bu* (pee-ah-rue buu)

public utilities – *kōeki jigyō* (koe-ay-kee jee-g'yoe)

public works – *kōkyō jigyō* (koe-k'yoe jee-g'yoe)

publish – *hakkan suru* (hock-kahn sue-rue), *shuppan
suru* (shuup-pahn sue-rue)

publisher – *shuppansha* (shuup-pahn-shah)

pulse – *parusu* (pah-rue-sue); *myaku* (m'yah-kuu)

purchase – *kōnyū suru* (cone-yuu sue-rue); *kau* (cow)

purchase order – *kōnyū sashizu sho* (cone-yuu sah-
she-zuu show)

purchase order (for securities) – *kai chūmon* (kye
chew-moan)

purchase price – *shi-ire kakaku* (she-ee-ray kah-kah-kuu)

purchasing agent – *kōbai gakari* (koe-by gah-kah-ree)

purchasing manager – *kōbai shunin* (koe-by shuu-neen)

purchasing power – *kōbai ryoku* (koe-by rio-kuu)

pyramid selling – *maruchi shōhō* (mah-rue-chee show-hoe)

— Q —

qualifications – *shikaku* (she-kah-kuu)

quality – *hinshitsu* (heen-sheet-sue)

Quality is very important to Japanese consumers.
Nihon-jin no shōhi sha ni totte hinshitsu wa taisetsu na koto desu.
(nee-hone-jeen no show-he shah ni tote-tay heen-sheet-sue wa tie-say-t'sue nah koe-toe dess)

quality control – *hinshitsu kanri* (heen-sheet-sue kahn-ree)

quality control circle – *kyū shii sākuru* (cue she-ee sah-kuu-rue)

quality goods – *yūryō hin* (yuu-rio heen)

quantity (number) – *sūryō* (sue-rio); (amount) *bunryō* (boon-rio)

quantity discount – *sūryō waribiki* (sue-rio wah-ree-bee-kee)

Will you give me a quantity discount?
Sūryō waribiki wo shite moraemasu ka?
(sue-rio wah-ree-bee-kee oh shtay moe-rye-mahss kah)

quantity order – *tairyō chūmon* (tie-rio chew-moan)

quarterly (publication) – *kikanshi* (kee-kahn-she)

quasi-public company – *jun-kōkyō kigyō-tai* (june-koe-k'yoe kee-g'yoe-tie)

question – *shitsumon* (sheet-sue-moan)

Does anyone have any questions?
Dare ka shitsumon ga arimasu ka?
(dah-ray kah sheet-sue-moan gah ah-ree-mahss kah)

quit-claim deed – *kenri hōki shōsho* (ken-ree hoe-kee show-show)

quorum – *teisū* (tay-sue)

quota – *wariate gaku* (wah-ree-ah-tay gah-kuu); *kuōta* (kuu-oh-tah)

quota system – *wariate sei* (wah-ree-ah-tay say)

quotation – *sōba* (so-bah)

What is today's quotation?

Kyō no sōba wa nan desu ka?

(k'yoe no so-bah wah nahn dess kah)

— R —

race (contest) – *kyōsō* (k'yoe-so)

race (human) – *jinshu* (jeen-shuu)

radar – *rēdā* (ray-dah)

radial tire – *rajiaru taiya* (rah-jee-ah-rue tie-yah)

radiator – *rajiēta* (rah-jee-ay-tah)

radio – *rajio* (rah-jee-oh)

radio cassette player – *rajikase* (rah-jee-kah-say)

railroad – *tetsudō* (tay-t'sue-doe)

rail shipment – *tetsudō yusō* (tay-t'sue-doe yuu-so)

rain check – *hikikae ken* (he-kee-kye ken)

raise – *ageru* (ah-gay-rue)

raise capital – *shikin chōtatsu* (she-keen choe-tot-sue)

rally – *hantō* (hahn-toe)

RAM – *zuiji kakikomi yomidashi memorii* (zuu-ee-jee kah-kee-koe-me yoe-me-dah-she may-moe-ree)

random access memory – *randamu akusesu memorii* (rahn-dah-muu ah-kuu-say-sue may-moe-ree)

random sample – *musakui chūshutsu mihon* (muu-sah-kuu-ee chew-shoot-sue me-hone)

rank (military) – *kaikyū* (kye-cue)

rate – *ritsu* (ree-t'sue); *wariai* (wah-ree-eye)

rate of exchange – *kawase sōba* (kah-wah-say so-bah)

rate of growth – *seichō ritsu* (say-choe ree-t'sue)

That company's rate of growth is very fast.

Sono kaisha no seichō ritsu wa taihen hayai desu. (so-no kye-shah no say-choe ree-t'sue wah tie-hen high-eye dess)

rate of increase – *zōka ritsu* (zoe-kah ree-t'sue)

rate of interest – *ri ritsu* (ree ree-t'sue)

rate of return – *shūeki ritsu* (shuu-ay-kee ree-t'sue)

ratio – *hiritsu* (he-ree-t'suc)
ration – *haikyū suru* (high-cue sue-rue)
raw materials – *gen zairyō* (gen zye-rio)
reaction (response) – *hannō* (hahn-no); *henji* (hen-jee)
 I will wait for your response.
  Anata no go-henji wo o-machi shimasu.
  (ah-nah-tah no go-hen-jee oh oh-mah-chee she-
  mahss)
ready cash – *sokkin barai* (soak-keen bah-rye)
ready-to-wear – *kisei fuku* (kee-say fuu-kuu)
real estate – *fudōsan* (fuu-doe sahn)
real income – *jisshitsu shotoku* (jee-sheet-sue show-
 toe-koe)
reality – *genjitsu* (gen-jee-t'sue)
real price – *jisshitsu kakaku* (jee-sheet-sue kah-kah-
 kuu)
real thing (genuine) – *genbutsu* (gen-boot-sue)
real time – *rearu taimu* (ray-ah-rue tie-muu)
real wages – *jisshitsu chingin* (jee-sheet-sue cheen-
 gheen)
reasonable care – *tōzen no chūi* (toe-zen no chew-ee)
rebate on sales – *harai modoshi* (hah-rye moe-doe-
 she)
recapitalization – *shihon saikōsei* (she-hone sigh-koe-
 say)
receipt – *uketori shō* (uu-kay-toe-ree-sho); *ryōshū shō*
 (rio-shuu show)
 A receipt, please.
  Ryōshū shō onegai shimasu.
  (rio-shuu show oh-nay-guy she-mahss)
recession – *keiki kōtai* (kay-kee koe-tie)
rechargeable – *sai-jūden kanō no* (sigh-juu-den kah-
 no no)
reciprocal trade – *gokei bōeki* (go-kay boe-ay-kee)
recommend – *suisen* (sue-ee-sen)

Can you recommend that company?
> *Sono kaisha wo suisen dekimasu ka?*
> (so-no kye-shah oh sue-ee-sen day-kee-mahss kah)

record player – *rekōdo purēya* (ray-koe-doe puu-ray-yah)

recovery (economic) – *kaifuku* (kye-fuu-kuu)

recovery of expenses – *hiyō no tori modoshi* (he-yoe-no toe-ree moe-doe-she)

rectifier – *seiryū-ki* (say-r'yuu-kee)

recur – *kurikaesu* (kuu-ree-kye-sue)

red figure (as in the red) – *aka ji* (ah-kah jee)

red tape – *o-yakusho shigoto* (oh-yahk-show she-go-toe)

re-export – *sai-yushutsu* (sigh-yuu-shoot-sue)

reference – *mimoto shōmei sho* (me-moe-toe show-may show)

reference, for your – *sankō ni naru* (sahn-koe nee nah-rue)

reference number – *shōgō bangō (show-go bahn-go)*

refinance – *rifainansu* (ree-fie-nahn-sue)

reflex camera – *refurekkusu kamera* (ray-fuu-rake-suu kah-may-rah)

refund – *harai modoshi* (hah-rye moe-doe-she)
I have not yet received a refund.
> *Harai modoshi wo mada moratteimasen.*
> (hah-rye moe-doe-she oh mah-dah moe-raht-tay-mah-sen)

refuse acceptance – *hikiuke wo kyozetsu suru* (he-kee-uu-kay oh k'yoe-zay-t'sue sue-rue)

refuse payment – *shiharai wo kyozetsu suru* (she-hah-rye oh k'yoe-zay-t'sue sue-rue)

register (patent, etc) – *tōroku suru* (toe-roe-kuu sue-rue)

registered agent – *kokyaku gakari* (koe-k'yah-kuu gah-kah-ree)

registered check – *rejisutādo chekku* (ray-jeece-tah-doe check-kuu)

registered design – *tōroku ishō* (toe-roe-kuu ee-show)

registered mail – *kakitome yūbin* (kah-kee-toe-may yuu-bean)

registered securities – *kimei shōken* (kee-may show-ken)

registered trademark – *tōroku shōhyō* (toe-roe-kuu show-h'yoe)

regular pay – *hon kyū* (hone cue)

regulation – *kisoku* (kee-so-kuu)

regulation (control) – *kitei* (kee-tay)

regulations (prospectus) – *kisoku sho* (kee-so-kuu show)

reimburse – *harai modosu* (hah-rye moe-doe-sue)

re-insurer – *sai-hoken sha* (sigh-hoe-ken shah)

remainder (sell off at discount) – *saisoku suru* (sigh-so-kuu sue-rue)

remedy (medical) – *chiryō hō* (chee-rio hoe)

remission of tax – *zei menjo* (zay men-joe)

remit money – *sōkin suru* (so-keen sue-rue)
  I will remit the money tomorrow.
   Ashita sōkin shimasu.
   (ah-shtah so-keen she-mahss)

remittance – *sōkin* (so-keen)

remodel – *kaizō* (kye-zoe)

remote control – *rimōto kontorōru* (ree-moe-toe cone-toe-roe-rue)

remuneration – *hōshū* (hoe-shuu)

renegotiate – *sai kōshō suru* (sigh koe-show sue-rue)
  I want to renegotiate my contract.
   Keiyaku wo saikōshō shitai no desu.
   (kay-yah-kuu oh sigh-koe-show she-tie no dess)

renew (subscription) – *keizoku suru* (kay-zoe-kuu sue-rue); *kōshin suru* (koe-sheen sue-rue)

renewal (renovate) – *kōshin* (koe-sheen)

renew contract – *keiyaku wo keizoku suru* (kay-yah-kuu oh kay-zoe-kuu sue-rue)

rent (obtain for a fee) – *kariru* (kah-ree-rue); rent paid for living quarters – *yachin* (yah-cheen)

rental (rented house) – *shaku-ya* (shah-kuu-yah); *kashi-ya* (kah-she-yah)

rent received (by landlord) – *chin-gashi ryō* (cheen-gah-she rio)

reorder – *sai-chūmon suru* (sigh-chew-moan sue-rue)

reorganize – *sai-hensei suru* (sigh-hen-say sue-rue)

repair – *naosu* (nah-oh-sue)

repairs – *shūri* (shuu-ree)

repay – *hensai suru* (hen-sigh sue-rue)

repeat order – *sai-chūmon* (sigh-chew-moan)

replace – *torikaeru* (toe-ree-kye-rue)

replacement – *torikae* (toe-ree-kye)

replacement costs – *shinpin torikae hi* (sheen-peen toe-ree-kye he)

replacement parts – *kōkan buhin* (koe-kahn buu-heen)

report (written) – *hōkoku sho* (hoe-koe-kuu show)

representative (agency, proxy) – *dairi* (dye-ree)

reproduction copy (for printing) – *kiyozuri* (kee-yoe-zuu-ree)

reproduction costs – *sai-seisan hi* (sigh-say-sahn he)

reputation – *hyōban* (h'yoe-bahn); have a good reputation – *hyōban ga ii* (h'yoe-bahn gah ee)

Does he (that person) have a good reputation?
   Sono hito wa hyōban ga ii desu ka?
   (so-no shtoe wah h'yoe-bahn gah ee dess kah)

request for bid – *nyūsatsu seikyū* (n'yuu-sah-t'sue say-cue)

requirement (demand, claim) – *yōkyū* (yoe-cue)

requirements – *hitsuyō jōken* (heat-sue-yoe joe-ken)

Please write down your requirements.

Hitsuyō jōken wo kaite kudasai.

(heat-sue yoe joe-ken oh kye-tay kuu-dah-sigh)

resale – *tenbai* (ten-by)

resale price – *sai-hanbai kakaku* (sigh-hahn-by kah-kah-kuu)

What is your resale price?

Sai-hanbai kakaku wa ikura desu ka?

(sigh-hahn-by kah-kah-kuu wah ee-kuu-rah dess kah)

research – *kenkyū* (ken-cue)

research department (room) – *kenkyū shitsu* (ken-cue sheet-sue)

research and development (R&D) – *kenkyū kaihatsu* (ken-cue kye-hot-sue)

research expenses – *kenkyū hi* (ken-cue he)

research institute – *kenkyū jo* (ken-cue joe)

reservation – *yoyaku* (yoe-yah-kuu)

I want to confirm my reservations.

Yoyaku wo kakunin shitai no desu.

(yoe-yah-kuu oh kah-kuu-neen she-tie no dess)

reserved (not aggressive or forward) – *enryo* (en-rio)

Don't be so shy (reserved).

Enryo shinaide kudasai.

(en-rio she-nigh-day kuu-dah-sigh)

reserves (money) – *junbi kin* (juum-bee keen)

resident buyer – *zaijū shiire nin* (zye-juu she-ee-ray neen)

residents (inhabitants, population) – *jūmin* (juu-meen)

resign – *jishoku suru* (jee-show-kuu sue-rue)

Mr. Baker resigned last year.

Beikā-san wa kyonen jishoku shimashita.

(bay-kah-sahn wah k'yoe-nen jee-show-kuu she-mah-shtah)

resolution (legal declaration) – *ketsugi* (kate-sue-ghee)

resort – *kōrakuchi* (koe-rah-kuu-chee)

resources – *shizai* (she-zye)

resources allocation – *shigen haibun* (she-gen high-boon)

respect – *sonkei suru* (soan-kay sue-rue)

responsibility – *sekinin* (say-kee-neen); take responsibility – *sekinin wo motsu* (say-kee-neen oh moat-sue)

responsible person – *sekinin sha* (say-kee-neen shah)
Who is the responsible person?
  Sekinin sha wa donata desu ka?
  (say-kee-neen shah wah doe-nah-tah dess kah)

restrictions – *seigen* (say-gen)

restrictions on exports – *yushutsu seigen* (yuu-shoot-sue say-gen)

restrictions on imports – *yunyū seigen* (yuun-yuu say-gen)

restrictions on trade – *bōeki seigen* (boe-ay-kee say-gen)

restrictive labor practices – *seigen-teki rōdō kanshū* (say-gen-tay-kee roe-doe kahn-shuu)

restructure – *sai-kōsei suru* (sigh-koe-say sue-rue)

results (consequences) – *kekka* (cake-kah)
Have the results come out (been announced)?
  Kekka wa mō demashita ka?
  (kay-kah wah moe day-mah-shtah kah)

resume (for job application) – *rireki sho* (ree-ray-kee show)

retail dealer – *kouri ten* (koe-uu-ree ten)

retail merchandise – *kouri shōhin* (koe-uu-ree show-heen)

retail outlet – *kouri ten* (koe-uu-ree ten)

retail price – *kouri nedan* (koe-uu-ree nay-dahn)

retail sales – *kouri* (koe-uu-ree)
What is the retail sales price?
  Kouri nedan wa nan desu ka?

(koe-uu-ree nay-dahn wah nahn dess kah)

retail sales tax – *kouri uriage zei* (koe-uu-ree uu-ree-ah-gay zay)

retail trade – *kouri gyō* (koe-uu-ree g'yoe)

retained earnings – *ryūho rieki* (r'yuu-hoe ree-ay-kee)

retainer (fee) – *komon ryō* (koe-moan rio); *konsarutanto ryō* (cone-sah-rue-tahn-toe rio)

retire – *taishoku suru* (tie-show-kuu sue-rue); *intai suru* (een-tie sue-rue)

retirement – *taishoku* (tie-show-kuu)

retirement age – *teinen* (tay-nen)

retirement fund – *taishoku kikin* (tie-show-kuu kee-keen)

retract – *torikesu* (toe-ree-kay-sue)

retroactive – *sakanobotte kōryoku wo hassuru* (sah-kah-no-boat-tay koe-r'yoe-kuu oh hah-sue-rue)

return on capital – *shihon shūeki* (she-hone shuu-ay-kee)

return on equity – *mochibun rieki-ritsu* (moe-chee-boon ree-ay-kee-ree-t'sue)

return on investment – *tōshi shūeki-ritsu* (toe-she shuu-ay-kee-ree-t'sue)

return on sales – *hanbai rieki ritsu* (hahn-by ree-ay-kee-ree-t'sue)

returns (unsold products) – *henpin* (hen-peen)

revenue – *shūnyū* (shuun-yuu); *shūeki* (shuu-ay-kee)

revenue bonds – *shūnyū tanpo sai* (shuun-yuu tahn-poe sigh)

revenue stamp – *shūnyū inshi* (shuun-yuu een-she)

revise – *shūsei suru* (shuu-say sue-rue); *teisei* (tay-say)

You must revise this contract.

Kono keiyaku wo shūsei shinakereba narimasen. (koe-no kay-yah-kuu oh shuu-say she-nah-kay-ray-bah nah-ree-mah-sen)

revision (alternation) – *kaisei* (kye-say)

revocable trust – *torikeshi kanō shintaku* (toe-ree-kay-she kah-no sheen-tah-kuu)

revolving credit – *kaiten shin'yō* (kye-ten sheen-yoe)

revolving fund – *kaiten shikin* (kye-ten she-keen)

revolving letter of credit – *kaiten shin'yō jō* (kye-ten sheen-yoe joe)

reward – *hōshū* (hoe-shuu)

rewrite – *kakikae* (kah-kee-kye)
I will rewrite the agreement by next week.
Raishū made ni kyōtei wo kakikaemasu.
(rye-shuu mah-day nee k'yoe-tay oh kah-kee-kye-mahss)

rich – *yūfuku na* (yuu-fuu-kuu nah)
Mr. Saito is very rich.
Saito-san wa taihen yūfuku desu.
(sigh-toe-sahn wah tie-hen yuu-fuu-kuu dess)

rider (stipulation on contract) – *tsuika jōkō* (t'sue-ee-kah joe-koe)

right of recourse – *shōkan seikyū ken* (show-kahn say-cue ken)

rise – *agaru* (ah-gah-rue)

rise in prices – *neage* (nay-ah-gay)
There has been a rise in prices.
Neage ga arimashita.
(nay-ah-gay gah ah-ree-mah-shtah)

risk (danger) – *kiken* (kee-ken)

risk analysis – *kiken bunseki* (kee-ken boon-say-kee)

risk assessment – *kiken satei* (kee-ken sah-tay)

risk capital – *kiken futan shihon* (kee-ken fuu-tahn she-hone)

rollback – *bukka hikisage seisaku* (buu-kah he-kee-sah-gay say-sah-kuu)

rolling stock – *sharyō* (shah-rio)

rollover (money) – *harai modoshi* (hah-rye moe-doe-she)

ROM – *yomidashi senyō memorii* (yoe-me-dah-she sen-yoe may-moe-ree)

rough draft – *shita gaki* (shtah gah-kee)

rough estimate – *gaisan mitsumori sho* (guy-sahn meet-sue-moe-ree show)

routine work – *kimari shigoto* (kee-mah-ree she-go-toe)

royalty (income from literary work, etc.) – *inzei* (een-zay)

royalty from patent – *tokkyo ken shiyō ryō* (toke-k'yoe ken she-yoe rio)

rule (regulation) – *kisoku* (kee-so-kuu)

rules of employment – *shūmu kisoku* (shuu-muu kee-so-kuu)

All employees must sign rules of employment.
> *Shain wa subete shūmu kisoku ni sain shinakereba narimasen.*
>
> (shah-een wah sue-bay-tay shuu-muu kee-so-kuu nee sign she-nah-kay-ray-bah nah-ree-mah-sen)

run short (of supplies/goods) – *fusoku suru* (fuu-so-kuu sue-rue)

rush – *isogu* (ee-so-guu)

rush order – *isogi no chūmon* (ee-so-ghee no chew-moan)

This is a rush order.
> *Kore wa isogi no chūmon desu.*
>
> (koe-ray wah ee-so-ghee no chew-moan dess)

— S —

safe; safety – *anzen* (ahn-zen)

safe-deposit box – *kashi kinko* (kah-she keen-koe); *anzen kinko* (ahn-zen keen-koe)

Please put this in the safe-deposit box.

> *Kore wa anzen kinko ni irete kudasai.*
> (koe-ray wah ahn-zen keen-koe nee ee-ray-tay kuu-dah-sigh)

safeguard (protection) – *hogo* (hoe-go)

safely – *buji ni* (buu-jee nee)

salaried worker – *sarariiman* (sah-rah-ree-mahn)

salary (monthly) – *gekkyū* (gay-cue); *kyūryō* (cue-rio); *sararii* (sah-rah-ree); salary increase – *shōkyū suru* (show-cue sue-rue)

salary based on efficiency, merit – *nōritsu-kyū* (no-ree-t'sue-cue)

sale – *uridashi* (uu-ree-dah-she); *sēru* (say-rue)

sales – *hanbai* (hahn-by); sales (by volume) – *uriage* (uu-ree-ah-gay)

sales analysis – *hanbai bunseki* (hahn-by boon-say-kee)

sales budget – *hanbai yosan* (hahn-by yoe-sahn)

The sales budget will be finished by Friday.

> *Hanbai yosan wa kin'yōbi made ni dekiagarimasu.*
> (hahn-by yoe-sahn wah keen-yoe-bee mah-day nee day-kee-ah-gah-ree-mahss)

sales engineer – *sērusu enjinia* (say-rue-sue en-jee-nee-ah)

sales estimate – *yosō uriage daka* (yoe-so uu-ree-ah-gay dah-kah)

sales force – *hanbai in* (hahn-by een)

sales forecasts – *hanbai yosoku* (hahn-by yoe-so-kuu)

sales management – *hanbai kanri* (hahn-by kahn-ree)

sales promotion – *hanbai sokushin* (hahn-by so-kuu-sheen)

sales quota – *hanbai wariate* (hahn-by wah-ree-ah-tay)

sales tax – *uriage zei* (uu-ree-ah-gay zay)

sales territory – *hanbai chiiki* (hahn-by chee-ee-kee)

sales turnover – *sō uriage daka* (so uu-ree-ah-gay dah-kah)

sales volume – *hanbai ryō* (hahn-by rio)

salvage – *kaishū suru* (kye-shuu sue-rue)

salvage charges – *kainan kyūjo hi* (kye-nahn cue-joe he)

sample – *mihon* (me-hone); take a sample – *mihon wo toru* (me-hone oh toe-rue)

sample line – *mihon shumoku* (me-hone shuu-moe-kuu)

sample size – *hyōhon no saizu* (h'yoe-hone no sigh-zuu)

sanctions – *seisai* (say-sigh)

sauna bath – *sauna* (sah-uu-nah); *mushi buro* (muu-she buu-roe)

save (put money into a checking account) – *chokin suru* (choe-keen sue-rue)

savings – *chochiku* (choe-chee-kuu)

savings account – *chochiku kanjō kōza* (choe-chee-kuu kahn-joe koe-zah)

savings bank – *chochiku ginkō* (choe-chee-kuu gheen-koe)

savings bonds – *chochiku saiken* (choe-chee-kuu sigh-ken)

scandal – *shūbun* (shuu-boon); *sukyandaru* (sue-k'yan-dah-rue)

schedule – *yotei* (yoe-tay)

What is your schedule tomorrow?
  Ashita no yotei wa dō desu ka?
  (ah-shtah no yoe-tay wah doe dess kah)

schedule for production – *seisan nittei* (say-sahn neat-tay)

scholarship – *shōgakukin* (show-gah-kuu-keen)

school clique – *gaku batsu* (gah-kuu bah-t'sue)

scientist – *kagakusha* (kah-gah-kuu-shah)

screening – *senbetsu kensa* (sen-bait-sue ken-sah)

seal (official registered name-stamp) – *inkan* (een-kahn); registerd name stamp – *jitsu-in* (jeet-sue-een); regular name stamp – *hanko* (hahn-koe)

sealed bid – *fūkan nyūsatsu* (fuu-kahn n'yuu-saht-t'sue)

search (investigate) – *sōsa* (so-sah); *sōsaku* (so-sah-kuu); *sagasu* (sah-gah-sue)

seasonal – *kisetsu-teki* (kee-say-t'sue-tay-kee)

seat (in vehicle) – *shiito* (she-toe)

seatbelt – *shiito beruto* (she-toe bay-rue-toe)

seat of honor (for guests or ranking people) – *kamiza* (kah-me-zah)

secondary offering for securities – *sai-uridashi* (sigh-uu-ree-dah-she)

secondary market for securities – *ryūtsū shijō* (r'yuu-t'sue she-joe)

second mortgage – *niban teitō* (nee-bahn tay-toe)

secret – *himitsu no* (he-meet-sue no)

secretary – *hisho* (he-show)

section chief/manager – *kachō* (kah-choe)

I have an appointment with section manager Tanaka.
  Tanaka kachō to yakusoku ga arimasu.
  (tah-nah-kah kah-choe toe yahk-so-kuu gah ah-ree-mahss)

secured accounts – *tanpo tsuki kanjō* (tahn-poe t'ski kahn-joe)

secured liability – *tanpo tsuki fusai* (tahn-poe t'ski
  fuu-sigh)
securities (bonds) – *yūka shōken* (yuu-kah show-ken)
security (financial) – *antei* (ahn-tay)
security (mortgage, guarantee) – *tanpo* (tahn-poe)
security pact – *anzen hoshō* (ahn-zen hoe-show)
self-confidence – *jishin* (jee-sheen)
self-employed – *jiei shiteiru* (jee-ay shtay-rue)
self-service – *serufu sābisu* (say-rue-fuu sah-bee-sue)
sell – *uru* (uu-rue); make a sale – *urikomu* (uu-ree-koe-
  muu)
sell direct – *chokusetsu uru* (choke-say-t'sue uu-rue)
semiconductor – *handōtai* (hahn-doe-tie)
send – *haken suru* (hah-ken sue-rue)
senior in position – *senpai* (sem-pie)
  Is Mr. Kanda your senior?
    Kanda-san wa anata no senpai desu ka?
      (kahn-dah-sahn wah ah-nah-tah no sem-pie dess
      kah)
seniority – *sennin ken* (sen-neen ken)
seniority system – *nenkō joretsu sei* (nen-koe joe-rate-
  sue say)
sensational – *senjōteki* (sen-joe-tay-kee)
sensor – *sensa* (sen-sah)
sequential control – *shikensu seigyo* (she-ken-sue
  say-g'yoe)
service (as in waiting on someone in a store) – *toriatsukai* (toe-ree-ah-t'sue-kye); *sābisu* (sah-bee-sue)
service area allowance – *kinmuchi teate* (keen-muu-
  chee tay-ah-tay)
service charge – *sābisu ryō* (sah-bee-sue rio)
service contract – *teiki tenken keiyaku* (tay-kee ten-
  ken kay-yah-kuu)
settle accounts – *kessan suru* (case-sahn sue-rue)
settlement (of accounts) – *kessan* (case-sahn)

settlement – *kaiketsu* (kye-kate-sue)

settlement in full – *sō kessan* (so case-sahn)

several – *ikutsuka no* (ee-coot-sue-kah no)

severance pay (retirement pay) – *taishoku kin* (tie-show-kuu keen)

shape – *katachi* (kah-tah-chee)

share (stock) – *kabu* (kah-buu); *kabushiki* (kah-buu-she-kee)

I want to buy some Sony stock.
  Sony no kabu wo kaitai desu.
  (sony no kah-buu oh kye-tie dess)

shareholder – *kabu nushi* (kah-buu nuu-she)

shareholder's equity – *kabu nushi mochibun* (kah-buu nuu-she moe-chee-boon)

shareholder's meeting – *kabu nushi kai* (kah-buu nuu-she kye)

shift (take turns) – *kōtai* (koe-tie)

shift work – *jikan kōtai no shigoto* (jee-kahn koe-tie no she-go-toe)

ship fare – *unchin* (uun-cheen)

shipment – *shukka* (shuke-kah)

shipper – *ni nushi* (nee nuu-she)

shipping (forwarding) – *shukka suru* (shuke-kah sue-rue)

shipping agent – *funagaisha dairiten* (fuu-nah-guy-shah dye-ree-ten)

shipping charges – *funazumi hi* (fuu-nah-zuu-me he)

shipping instructions – *funazumi sashizu sho* (fuu-nah-zuu-me sah-she-zuu show)

shipping strike – *kaiun sutoraiki* (kye-uun sue-toe-rye-kee)

shop (store) – *mise* (me-say); stand, stall – *baiten* (by-ten)

shopping – *kaimono* (kye-moe-no); *shoppingu* (shope-peen-guu)

shopping center – *shoppingu senta* (shope-peen-guu sen-tah)

shortage (deficiency) – *fusoku* (fuu-so-kuu)

short delivery – *ukewatashi daka busoku* (uu-kay-wah-tah-she dah-kah buu-so-kuu)

short of – *fusoku shiteiru* (fuu-so-kuu shtay-rue)

short shipment – *tsumi nokoshi hin* (t'sue-me no-koe-she heen)

short-term capital account – *tanki shihon kanjō* (tahn-kee she-hone kahn-joe)

short-term debt – *tanki fusai* (tahn-kee fuu-sigh)

short-term financing – *tanki yūshi* (tahn-kee yuu-she)

shrink-wrapping – *shūshuku hōsō* (shuu-shuu-kuu hoe-so)

sick leave – *yūkyū byōki kyūka* (yuu-cue b'yoe-kee cue-kah)

sight draft – *ichiran barai kawase tegata* (ee-chee-rahn bah-rye kah-wah-say tay-got-tah)

signature – *shomei* (show-may)
  Where do I sign?
  Doko ni shomei shimasu ka?
  (doe-koe nee show-may she-mahss kah)

silent partner – *gyōmu wo tantō shinai shain* (g'yoe-muu oh tahn-toe she-nigh shah-een)

simulate – *maneru* (mah-nay-rue)

sing – *utau* (uu-tah-uu)
  I will sing.
  Utaimasu.
  (uu-tie-mahss)
  Even when I'm drunk I can't sing.
  Yotte mo utaemasen.
  (yote-tay moe uu-tah-ay-mah-sen)

sinking fund – *gensai kikin* (gen-sigh kee-keen)

size – *saizu* (sigh-zuu)

skilled labor – *jukuren rōdō* (juu-kuu-ren roe-doe)

slide (photo) – *suraido* (sue-rye-doe)

slide projector – *suraido eisha-ki* (sue-rye-doe ay-shah-kee)

sliding scale – *suraido sei* (sue-rye-doe say)

slump – *keiki chintai* (kay-kee cheen-tie)

small business – *shō kigyō* (show kee-g'yoe)

smoke (tobacco) – *tabako wo sū* (tah-bah-koe oh sue); no smoking – *kin'en* (kee-en)

May I smoke in here?
Tabako ii desu ka?
(tah-bah-koe ee dess kah)

Would you please not smoke. I have an allergy.
Arerugii na no de. Tabako go-enryo negaimasu ka?
(ah-ray-rue-ghee nah no day tah-bah-koe go-en-rio nay-guy-mahss ka)

social expenses – *kōsai-hi* (koe-sigh he)

socialize – *otsukiai suru* (oat-ski-eye sue-rue)

softcover (book) – *kami-byōshi bon* (kah-me-b'yoe-she bone); *pēpabakku* (pay-pah back-kuu)

soft goods – *orimono rui* (oh-ree-moe-no rue-ee)

soft loan – *sofuto rōn* (so-fuu-toe roan)

soft sell – *odayaka na shōhō* (oh-dah-yah-kah no show-hoe)

software – *sofutowea* (so-fuu-toe-way-ah)

sole agent – *sō dairiten* (so dye-ree-ten)

Mitsui Norin is our sole agent.
Mitsui Norin wa uchi no sō dairiten desu.
(meet-sue-ee no-reen wah uu-chee no soh dye-ree-ten dess)

sole rights – *dokusen ken* (doke-sen ken)

solvency (financially) – *shiharai nōryoku* (she-hah-rye no-rio-kuu)

soybeans – *daizu* (dye-zuu)

Are you importing soybeans from America?

Amerika hara daizu wo yunyū shite imasu ka?
(ah-may-ree-kah kah-rah dye-zuu oh yune-yuu
shtay ee-mahss kah)

space (area) – *kūkan* (kuu-kahn); space (as in outer) –
uchū (uu-chew)

speaker (electronic) – *supiika* (spee-kah)

special – *tokushu* (toke-shuu); *tokubetsu* (toe-kuu-bait-
sue)

special characteristics (special points) – *tokuchō*
(toke-choe)

special delivery mail – *sokutatsu* (so-kuu-tot-sue)
Please send this (mail) special delivery.
Kore wo sokutatsu ni shite kudasai.
(koe-ray oh so-kuu-tot-sue nee shtay kuu-dah-sigh)

special feature article – *tokushū* (toke-shuu)

special idiosyncrasy – *tokusei* (toke-say)

specialist – *senmonka* (sem-moan-kah); specialize –
senmonteki na (sem-moan-tay-kee nah)

special (unique) products – *tokusan* (toke-sahn);
special regional/area products – *meibutsu* (may-boot-
sue)

specialty goods – *senmon hin* (sem-moan heen)

speculation – *okusoku* (oh-kuu-so-kuu)

speech – *enzetsu* (en-zay-t'sue)

speedometer – *sokudo-kei* (so-kuu-doe-kay)

spoilage – *shison hin* (she-soan heen)

spot delivery – *genba watashi* (gen-bah wah-tah-she)

spot market – *genbutsu shijō* (gen-boot-sue she-joe)

spreadsheet – *supureddo shiito* (sue-prayed-doe she-
toe)

Spring Wage Offensive – *shuntō* (shune-toe)

square deal – *kōhei torihiki* (koe-hay toe-ree-he-kee)

stable – *antei* (ahn-tay); stabilize – *antei suru* (ahn-tay
sue-rue)

staff (staff member) – *shokuin* (show-kuu-een)

staff assistant – *sutaffu ashisutanto* (stuff-fuu ah-sheece-tahn-toe)

staff organization – *sutaffu soshiki* (stuff-fuu so-she-kee)

stage (step) – *dankai* (dahn-kye)

stalemate – *kōchaku jōtai* (koe-chah-kuu joe-tie)

standard – *kijun* (kee-june)

standard (average) – *hyōjun* (h'yoe-june); average quality – *hyōjun no seishitsu* (h'yoe-june no say-sheet-sue)

standard costs – *hyōjun genka* (h'yoe-june gen-kah)

standard equipment – *hyōjun sōbi-hin* (h'yoe-june so-bee-heen)

standardization – *kikaku-ka* (kee-kah-kuu-kah)

standardized products – *kikaku hin* (kee-kah-kuu heen)

standard of living – *seikatsu suijun* (say-cot-sue sue-ee-june)

standard practice – *hyōjun kankō* (h'yoe-june kahn-koe)

standard product – *hyōjun hin* (h'yoe-june heen)

standard time – *hyōjun ji* (h'yoe-june jee)

standing charges – *kotei hi* (koe-tay he)

standing costs – *kotei hi* (koe-tay he)

standing order – *keizoku sashizu sho* (kay-zoe-kuu sah-she-zuu show)

stapler – *hochikisu* (hoe-chee-kee-sue)
  Loan me your stapler for a second.
    Hochikisu wo chotto kashite kudasai.
    (hoe-chee-kee-sue oh choe-toe kahsh-tay kuu-dah-sigh)

start-up costs – *sōgyō kaishi keihi* (so-g'yoe kye-she kay-he)

statement of accounts – *kanjō sho* (kahn-joe show); *kessan hōkoku sho* (case-sahn hoe-koe-kuu show)

statistics – *tōkei* (toe-kay)

statute – *hōrei* (hoe-ray)

statute of limitations – *jikō hō* (jee-koe hoe)

steel mill – *seitetsu sho* (say-tay-t'sue show)

steering wheel – *handoru* (hahn-doe-rue)

step (stage, grade) – *dankai* (dahn-kye)

stereo TV – *sutereo terebi* (sue-tay-ray-oh tay-ray-bee)

stock (shares) – *kabu* (kah-buu)

stockbroker – *kabushiki nakagai nin* (kah-buu-she-kee nah-kah-guy neen)

stock certificate – *kabu ken* (kah-buu ken)

stock company – *kabushiki gaisha* (kah-buu-she-kee guy-shah)

stock control – *zaiko hin kanri* (zye-koe heen kahn-ree)

stock exchange – *kabushiki torihiki sho* (kah-buu-she-kee toe-ree-he-kee show)

stockholder – *kabu nushi* (kah-buu nuu-she)

stockholder's equity – *kabu nushi mochibun* (kah-buu nuu-she moe-chee-boon)

stock index – *kabuka shisū* (kah-buu-kah she-sue)

stock market – *kabushiki shijō* (kah-buu-she-kee she-joe)

stock option – *sutokku opushon* (stoke-kuu oh-puu-shone)

stock portfolio – *kabushiki tōshi haibun hyō* (kah-buu-she-kee toe-she high-boon h'yoe)

stock split –- *kabushiki bunkatsu* (kah-buu-she-kee boon-cot-sue)

stock turnover (securities) – *kabushiki kaiten-ritsu* (kah-buu-she-kee kye-ten-ree-t'sue)

stop-loss order – *gyaku sashine chūmon* (g'yah-kuu sah-she-nay chew-moan)

storage – *sōko hokan* (so-koe hoe-kahn)

storehouse (warehouse) – *sōko* (so-koe)

stress – *sutoresu* (stow-ray-sue)

stress management – *sutoresu kanri* (stow-ray-sue kahn-ree)

strike – *sutoraiki* (stow-rye-kee); *suto* (stow)

strikebreaker – *suto yaburi* (stow yah-buu-ree)

strong – *tsuyoi* (t'sue-yoe-ee); (intense) *kyōretsu na* (k'yoe-ray-t'sue nah); (durable) *jōbu na* (joe-buu nah)

structure – *soshiki* (so-she-kee)

subcontract – *shitauke ni dasu* (shtah-uu-kay nee dah-sue)

subcontractor – *shitauke gyōsha* (shtah-uu-kay g'yoe-shah)

subject (topic) – *wadai* (wah-dye); *mondai* (moan-dye)

sublet space – *tentai* (ten-tie)

subscribe – *yoyaku suru* (yoe-yah-kuu sue-rue)

subscriber – *kōdokusha* (koe-doke-shah)

subscription – *kōdoku* (koe-doe-kuu)

subscription price – *yoyaku kin* (yoe-yah-kuu keen)

submit a bid – *nyūsatsu suru* (nuu-sah-t'sue sue-rue)

subsidiary – *ko gaisha* (koe guy-shah)

subsidy – *hojo kin* (hoe-joe keen)

substandard – *hyōjun ika no* (h'yoe-june ee-kah no)

subtle – *bimyō na* (beam-yoe nah)

suburb – *kōgai* (koe-guy)

  Do you live in the suburbs?

   Kōgai ni sunde imasu ka?

   (koe-guy nee soon-day ee-mahss kah)

subway – *chikatetsu* (chee-kah-tay-t'sue)

  Is there a subway?

   Chikatetsu ga arimasu ka?

   (chee-kah-tay-t'sue gah ah-ree-mahss kah)

  Let's go by subway.

   Chikatetsu de ikimashō.

   (chee-kah-tay-t'sue day ee-kee-mah-show)

succeed – *seikō suru* (say-koe sue-rue)

sum of money – *kingaku* (keen-gah-kuu); sum total – *zen gaku* (zen gah-kuu)

summarize – *tekiyō suru* (tay-kee-yoe sue-rue)

summary (outline) – *taiyō* (tie-yoe)

sundry (miscellaneous goods) – *zakka* (zahk-kah)

supervisor – *kantoku sha* (kahn-toe-kuu-shah)

supplement (publication) – *bessatsu* (base-sah-t'sue)

supplier – *kyōkyū sha* (k'yoe-cue shah)

supplies – *shizai* (she-zye)

supply and demand – *kyōkyū to juyō* (k'yoe-cue toe juu-yoe)

supply department – *shizai bu* (she-zye buu)

support activities – *shien katsudō* (she-en cot-sue-doe)

surcharge – *fuka kin* (fuu-kah keen)
Will there be a surcharge?
Fuka kin ga arimasu ka?
(fuu-kah keen gah ah-ree-mahss kah)

surplus capital – *shihon jōyo kin* (she-hone joe-yoe keen)

surplus goods – *jōyo hin* (joe-yoe heen)

surtax – *fuka zei* (fuu-kah zay)

suspend payment – *shiharai teishi suru* (she-hah-rye tay-she sue-rue)

switch – *suitchi* (sue-ee-chee)

sworn statement – *sensei chinjutsu sho* (sen-say cheen-jute-sue show)

symposium – *zadankai* (zah-dahn-kye)

syndicate – *shinjikēto* (sheen-jee-kay-toe)

syndicate a project – *shinjikēto wo tsukuru* (sheen-jee-kay-toe oh t'sue-kuu-rue)

synthetic (material) – *gōsei no* (go-say no)

system – *seido* (say-doe); *shisutemu* (she-stay-muu)
What system do you think is best?
Dono seido ga ichiban ii to omoimasu ka?

    (doe-no say-doe gah ee-chee-bahn ee toe oh-moe-ee-mahss kah)

system analysis – *seido bunseki* (say-doe boon-say-kee)

systematic (methodical) – *soshiki-teki na* (so-she-kee-tay-kee nah)

systems design – *shisutemu sekkei* (she-stay-muu sake-kay)

systems engineering – *shisutemu enjiniaringu* (she-stay-muu en-jee-nee-ah-reen-guu)

systems management – *shisutemu kanri* (she-stay-muu kahn-ree).

— T —

table of contents – *mokuji* (moe-kuu-jee)
tactics – *senjutsu* (sen-jute-sue)
tag (product label) – *raberu* (rah-bay-rue)
take-home pay – *te-dori kyūryō* (tay-doe-ree cue-rio)
  My take-home pay is not enough to go around.
   *Watakushi no te-dori kyūryō wa jūbun dewa
   arimasen.*
   (wah-tock-she no tay-doe-ree cue-rio wah juu-boon
   day-wah ah-ree-mah-sen)
takeover – *nottori* (note-toe-ree)
tangible assets – *yūkei shisan* (yuu-kay she-sahn)
tanker – *tanka* (tahn-kah)
tape – *tēpu* (tay-puu)
tape recorder – *tepu rekōda* (tay-puu ray-koe-dah)
target (for sales, etc) – *mokuhyō* (moe-kuu-h'yoe)
target price – *mokuhyō kakaku* (moe-kuu-h'yoe kah-
  kah-kuu)
tariff – *kanzei* (kahn-zay)
tariff barriers – *kanzei shōheki* (kahn-zay show-hay-
  kee)
tariff classification – *kanzei tōkyū bunrui* (kahn-zay
  toe-cue boon-rue-ee)
tariff differential – *kanzei ritsu kakusa* (kahn-zay
  ree-t'sue kah-kuu-sah)
tariff rate (tax) – *zei ritsu* (zay ree-t'sue)
tariff war – *kanzei sen* (kahn-zay sen)
task force – *tasuku fōsu* (tahss-kuu foe-sue)
tax – *zeikin* (zay-keen)
tax allowance – *zei kōjo* (zay koe-joe)
taxation – *kazei* (kah-zay)
tax base – *kazei hyōjun* (kah-zay h'yoe-june)

tax burden – *sozei futan* (so-zay fuu-tahn)

tax business – *zeimu* (zay-muu)

tax collector – *shūzei kan* (shuu-zay kahn)

tax deduction – *zei kōjo* (zay koe-joe)

tax evasion – *datsu zei* (dot-sue zay)

tax-free income – *hika zei shotoku* (he-kah zay show-toe-kuu)

tax haven – *kei kazei koku* (kay kah-zay koe-kuu)

taxi – *takushii* (tahk-she)
  Please call a taxi (for me).
    Takushii wo yonde kudasai.
    (tahk-she oh yoan-day kuu-dah-sigh)

tax office – *zeimusho* (zay-muu-show)

tax relief – *sozei keigen* (so-zay kay-gen)

tax shelter – *zeikin hinan shudan* (zay-keen he-nahn shuu-dahn)

technical knowhow – *gijutsu* (ghee-jute-sue)

technical tie-up – *gijutsu teikei* (ghee-jute-sue tay-kay)

telecommunications – *terekomyunikēshon* (tay-ray-koe-muu-nee-kay-shone)

telegram – *denshin* (den-sheen); *denpō* (den-poe)

television – *terebi* (tay-ray-bee)

telex – *terekkusu* (tay-rake-kuu-sue)

teller (bank) – *kinsen suitō gakari* (keen-sen sweet-oh gah-kah-ree)

temporary – *kari no* (kah-ree no); *ichiji-teki* (ee-chee-jee-tay-kee)

temporary employment – *rinji yatoi* (reen-jee yah-toe-ee)

ten-thousand-yen note – *ichi-man-en satsu* (ee-chee-mahn-en sah-t'sue)

terminal (computer) – *tāminaru* (tah-me-nah-rue)

terminate – *haishi suru* (high-she sue-rue)

term insurance – *teiki hoken* (tay-kee hoe-ken)

term loan – *kigen-tsuki kariire-kin* (kee-gen-t'ski kah-ree-ee-ray-keen)

terms of sale – *hanbai jōken* (hahn-by joe-ken)

terms of trade – *kōeki jōken* (koe-ay-kee joe-ken)

terrible – *hidoi* (he-doy)

territorial waters – *ryōkai* (rio-kye)

territory – *chiiki* (chee-ee-kee)

thanks for your efforts – *otsukare-sama* (oh-t'sue-kah-ray-sah-mah)

that (thing, topic) – *rei no* (ray no)

theme – *shudai* (shuu-dye); *tēma* (tay-mah)

thermostat – *sāmosuttato* (sah-moe-staht-toe)

through bill of lading – *tōshi funani shōken* (toe-she fuu-nah-nee show-ken)

ticker tape (for stocks) – *kabushiki sōba hyōji tēpu* (kah-buu-she-kee so-bah h'yoe-jee tay-puu)

tie-up – *teikei suru* (tay-kay sue-rue)
  I would like to tie-up with a medium-sized Japanese company.
  Chū gurai no Nihon no kaisha to teikei shitai desu.
  (chew guu-rye no nee-hone no kye-shah toe tay-kay she-tie dess)

tight market – *kinshuku shikyō* (keen-shuu-kuu she-k'yoe)

tight with money (stingy) – *kechi* (kay-chee)

time and motion study – *sagyō jikan sagyō dōsa sōkan kenkyū* (sah-g'yoe jee-kahn sah-g'yoe doe-sah so-kahn ken-cue)

time deposit – *teiki yokin* (tay-kee yoe-keen)

time difference – *jisa* (jee-sah)

time-sharing – *taimu shearingu* (tie-muu shay-ah-een-guu)

timetable – *jikan hyō* (jee-kahn h'yoe)

time zone – *jikan tai* (jee-kahn tie)

tip (gratuity) – *chippu* (cheap-puu)

tip (inside information) – *insaido infomēshon* (in-sigh-doe in-foe-may-shone)

tire – *taiya* (tie-yah)

title (of book, article) – *hyōdai* (h'yoe-dye); *daimei* (dye-may)

title (of company manager/executive) – *katagaki* (kah-tah-gah-kee)

title to (power over) – *kengen* (ken-gen)

toast (in celebration) – *shukuhai* (shuu-kuu-high); to give a toast – *shukuhai wo ageru* (shuu-kuu-high oh ah-gay-rue)

Tokyo Chamber of Commerce & Industry – *Tōkyō Shōkō Kaigisho* (toe-k'yoe show-koe kye-ghee-show)

tonnage – *yōseki ton sū* (yoe-say-kee tone sue)

tools – *dōgu* (doe-guu)

We (I) do not have the necessary tools.
Hitsuyō na dōgu wo motteimasen.
(heat-sue-yoe nah doe-guu oh moat-tay-mah-sen)

too soon – *hayasugiru* (hah-yah-sue-ghee-ree)

topic – *wadai* (wah-dye)

top management – *saikō keiei sha* (sigh-koe kay-ay shah)

top price – *saikō kakaku* (sigh-koe kah-kah-kuu)

top quality – *saikō hinshitsu* (sigh-koe heen-sheet-sue)

total – *sōkei* (so-kay)

total quality control (TQC) – *Tii Kyu Shii* (tea-cue-she)

total sum – *sō gaku* (so gah-kuu)

trade (business) – *torihiki* (toe-ree-he-kee)

trade agreement – *bōeki kyōtei* (boe-ay-kee k'yoe-tay)

trade and commerce – *tsūshō* (t'sue-show)

trade association – *gyōkai* (g'yoe-kye); *shōgyō kumiai* (show-g'yoe kuu-me-eye)

trade barrier – *bōeki shōheki* (boe-ay-kee show-hay-kee)

trade commission – *bōeki iinkai* (boe-ay-kee ee-een-kye)

trade credit – *torihiki saki shin'yō* (toe-ree-he-kee sah-kee sheen-yoe)

trade discount – *gyōsha waribiki* (g'yoe-shah wah-ree-bee-kee)

trade friction – *bōeki masatsu* (boe-ay-kee mah-saht'sue)

trademark – *shirushi* (she-rue-she); *tōroku shōhyō* (toe-roe-kuu show-h'yoe)

trade mission – *tsūshō shisetsu* (t'sue-show she-say-t'sue)

trade union – *rōdō kumiai* (roe-doe kuu-me-eye)

trading company – *shōji gaisha* (show-jee guy-shah); *bōeki gaisha* (boe-ay-kee guy-shah); *shōsha* (show-shah)

trading floor (exchange) – *tachiai jō* (tah-chee-eye joe)

train (educate) – *kunren suru* (coon-ren sue-rue)

trainee – *jisshū sei* (jeesh-shuu-say)

transaction – *torihiki* (toe-ree-he-kee)

transfer (money) – *furikae* (fuu-ree-kye)

transfer by computer – *tensō* (ten-so)

translate – *hon'yaku suru* (hone-yah-kuu sue-rue)
  Please translate this.
    Kore wo hon'yaku shite kudasai.
    (koe-ray oh hone-yah-kuu shtay kuu-dah-sigh)

translation – *yakubun* (yah-kuu-boon)

translator – *hon'yaku sha* (hone-yah-kuu shah)

transmission (vehicle) – *toransumisshon* (toe-rahns-meesh-shone)

transportation – *un'yū* (uun-yuu); *yusō* (yuu-so)

transportation charge – *unchin* (uun-cheen)

transportation expenses – *yusō hi* (yuu-so he)

transportation terminal – *shūten* (shuu-ten)

travel (trip) – *ryokō* (rio-koe); *tabi* (tah-bee)

travel expenses – *ryō hi* (rio he)

traveler's check – *ryokō kogitte* (rio-koe koe-gheet-tay)

Are traveler's checks acceptable?

Ryokō kogitte de yoroshii desu ka?
(rio-koe koe-gheet-tay day yoe-roe-she dess kah)

trend – *taisei* (tie-say); *keikō* (kay-koe); *dōkō* (doe-koe)

trial period – *shiyō kikan* (she-yoe kee-kahn)

trial use – *shiyō suru* (she-yoe sue-rue)

trouble-shoot – *mondai wo tsukitomete kaiketsu suru* (moan-dye oh t'ski-toe-may-tay kye-kate-sue sue-rue)

truck – *torakku* (toe-rahk-kuu)

truckload – *kashikiri kamotsu* (kah-she-kee-ree kah-moat-sue)

trust – *shin'yō* (sheen-yoe); problem of trust – *shin'yō mondai* (sheen-yoe moan-dye)

trust (financial institution) – *shintaku* (sheen-tah-kuu)

trust bank – *shintaku ginkō* (sheen-tah-kuu gheen-koe)

trustee – *jutaku sha* (juu-tah-kuu shah)

trust fund – *shintaku shikin* (sheen-tah-kuu she-keen)

tuner – *chūna* (chew-nah)

two-shift system – *ni-kōtai sei* (nee-koe-tie say)

type; kind – *shurui* (shuu-rue-ee)

How many kinds do you have?

Ikutsu shurui ga arimasu ka?
(ee-coot-sue shuu-rue-ee gah ah-ree-mahss kah)

— U —

ultimatum – *saigo no tsūchō* (sigh-go no t'sue-choe)
unaccompanied goods – *bessō nimotsu* (bay-so nee-moat-sue)
unanimously – *manjōitchi* (mahn-joe-eech-chee)
uncollectible accounts – *kogetsuki kanjō* (koe-gate-sue-kee kahn-joe)
undercapitalized – *tōshi busoku no* (toe-she buu-so-kuu no)
under consideration – *kentō chū* (ken-toe chew)
Your application is under consideration.
   Anata no mōshikomi wa ima kentō chū desu.
   (ah-nah-toe no moe-she-koe-me wah ee-mah ken-toe chew dess)
undercut (price) – *nedan wo kirisageru* (nay-dahn oh kee-ree-sah-gay-rue)
underdeveloped nations – *kōshin koku* (koe-sheen koe-kuu)
underestimate – *kashō hyōka suru* (kah-show h'yoe-kah sue-rue)
underpaid – *shiharai busoku no* (she-hah-rye buu-so-kuu no)
undersigned – *shomei sha* (show-may shah)
understanding (agreement) – *kyōtei* (k'yoe-tay)
understanding (comprehension) – *rikai* (ree-kye); *ryōkai* (rio-kye)
undervalue – *kashō hyōka suru* (kah-show h'yoe-kah sue-rue)
underwriter of insurance – *hoken gyōsha* (hoe-ken g'yoe-shah)
underwriter of securities – *hikiuke gyōsha* (he-kee-uu-kay g'yoe-shah)

unearned revenue – *furō shūnyū (fuu-roe shuun-yuu)*
unemployment – *shitsugyō* (sheet-sue-g'yoe)
unemployment compensation – *shitsugyō teate*
  (sheet-sue-g'yoe tay-ah-tay)
unexpected – *igai* (ee-guy); *yosōgai* (yoe-so-guy)
unfair (unreasonable) – *fu-kōhei na* (fuu-koe-hay nah)
  I believe those are unfair conditions.
    Sore wa fu-kōhei na jōken da to omoimasu.
    (so-ray wah fuu-koe-hay nah joe-ken dah toe oh-
    moe-ee-mahss)
unfair competition – *fu kōhei kyōsō* (fuu-koe-say
  k'yoe-so)
unfavorable – *furi na* (fuu-ree nah)
unfeasible – *jikkō fukanō na* (jee-koe fuu-kah-no nah)
union (labor) – *rōdō kumiai* (roe-doe kuu-me-eye);
  union member – *kumiai-in* (kuu-me-eye-een)
union contract – *rōdō keiyaku* (roe-doe kay-yah-kuu)
union label – *kumiai fuhyō* (kuu-me-eye fuu-h'yoe)
unique – *yuniiku* (yuu-nee-kuu); *yuiitsu no* (yuu-eat-
  sue no)
unit cost – *tan-i genka* (tahn-ee gen-kah)
unit price – *tanka* (tahn-kah)
universal (the whole world) – *zen-sekai no* (zen-say-
  kye no)
university – *daigaku* (dye-gah-kuu)
unlisted number – *hijōjō no bangō* (he-joe-joe no
  bahn-go)
unsecured liability – *mu-tanpo fusai* (muu-tahm-poe
  fuu-sigh)
unsecured loan – *shin'yō gashi* (sheen-yoe gah-she)
unskilled labor – *mi-jukuren rōdō* (me-juu-kuu-ren
  roe-doe)
unstable – *fuantei* (fuu-ahn-tay)
up to expectations – *kitai dōri ni* (kee-tie doe-ree nee)
upturn – *kōten* (koe-ten)

urgent business – *isogi no yō* (ee-so-ghee no yoe)
I have urgent business with Mr. Kato.
  Kato-san ni isogi no yō ga arimasu.
  (kah-toe-sahn nee ee-so-ghee no yoe gah ah-ree-mahss)

use – *shiyō* (she-yoe)

use tax – *shiyō zei* (she-yoe zay)

user-friendly – *yūzā furendorii* (yuu-zah fuu-ren-doe-ree)

utilities – *kōnetsu* (koe-nate-sue); utility expenses – *kōnetsu hi* (koe-nate-sue he)

— V —

vacation – *bekēshon* (bay-kay-shone); *kyūka* (cue-kah)

valid – *yūkō na* (yuu-koe nah)

validate – *yūkō to mitomeru* (yuu-koe to me-toe-may-rue)

valid for one year – *ichi-nen yūkō* (ee-chee-nen yuu-koe)

This document is valid for one year.

Kono shorui wa ichi-nen yūkō desu.

(koe-no show-rue-ee wah ee-chee-nen yuu-koe dess)

valuable – *neuchi ga aru* (nay-uu-chee gah ah-rue)

valuables – *kichōhin* (kee-choe-heen)

Do you have a safe for valuables?

Kichōhin no kinko ga arimasu ka?

(kee-choe-heen no keen-koe gah ah-ree-mahss kah)

valuation (financial) – *hyōka* (h'yoe-kah)

valuation (real estate) – *satei* (sah-tay)

value – *kachi* (kah-chee)

value-added tax – *fuka-kachi zei* (fuu-kah-kah-chee zay)

value, book – *chōbo kakaku* (choe-boe kah-kah-kuu)

value, face – *gakumen kakaku* (gah-kuu-men kah-kah-kuu)

value for duty – *zeigaku satei kakaku* (zay-gah-kuu sah-tay kah-kah-kuu)

variable annuity – *hengaku nenkin* (hen-gah-kuu nen-keen)

variable costs – *hendō hi* (hen-doe he)

variable import duty – *hendō yunyū fuka zei* (hen-doe yuun-yuu fuu-kah-zay)

variable rate – *hendō ritsu* (hen-doe ree-t'sue)

variety – *henka* (hen-kah); *iro-iro* (ee-roe-ee-roe)

vendor – *uri nushi* (uu-ree nuu-she)

vendor's lien – *uri nushi horyū ken* (uu-ree nuu-she hoe-r'yuu ken)

venture capital – *kiken futan shihon* (kee-ken fuu-tahn she-hone)

verification – *kenshō* (ken-show)

verify – *shōmei suru* (show-may sue-rue)
  Please verify this.
    Kore wo shōmei shite kudasai.
    (koe-ray oh show-may shtay kuu-dah-sigh)

vertical integration – *suichoku tōgō* (sue-ee-choe-kuu toe-go)

vested interest – *kitoku riken* (kee-toe-kuu ree-ken)

vested rights – *kitoku ken* (kee-toe-kuu ken)

veto – *kyohi ken* (k'yoe-he ken)

via (as in via Los Angeles) – *keiyu* (kay-yuu)

vice chief (vice director) – *jichō* (jee-choe)

vice-president – *fuku shachō* (fuu-kuu shah-choe)

video casette camera – *bideo kasetto kamera* (bee-day-oh kah-set-toe kah-may-rah)

video casette player – *bideo kasetto purēya* (bee-day-oh kah-set-toe puu-ray-yah)

video casette recorder – *bideo kasetto rekōda* (bee-day-oh kah-set-toe ray-koe-dah)

video disc – *bideo disuku* (bee-day-oh disk-uu)

video tape recorder – *bideo tēpu rekōda* (bee-day-oh tape-uu ray-koe-dah)

vinyl – *biniiru* (bee-nee-rue); made of vinyl – *biniiru-sei no* (bee-nee-rue-say no)

violation – *ihan* (ee-hahn)

VIP Room – *Bii-Ai-Pii rūmu* (bee-eye-pee rue-muu); *tokubetsu machiai shitsu* (toe-kuu-bait-sue mah-chee-eye sheet-sue)

visible balance of trade – *shōhin bōeki shūshi* (show-heen boe-ay-kee shu-she)

visitor – *hōmon-sha* (hoe-moan-shah); *okyaku-san* (oh-k'yahck-sahn)

volatile market – *kimagure shikyō* (kee-mah-guu-ray she-k'yoe)

volume – *ryō* (rio)

volume discount – *sūryō waribiki* (sue-rio wah-ree-bee-kee)

volume, sales – *hanbai ryō* (hahn-by rio)

vote – *tōhyō suru* (toe-h'yoe sue-rue)

voting rights – *tōhyō ken* (toe-h'yoe ken)

voucher – *denpyō* (den-p'yoe)

— W —

wage (income) – *chingin* (cheen-gheen); *kyūryō* (cue-rio)

wage based on job-position – *shokumu kyū* (show-kuu-muu cue)

wage based on seniority – *nenkō joretsu chingin* (nen-koe joe-rate-sue cheen-gheen)

wage differential – *chingin kakusa* (cheen-gheen kah-kuu-sah)

wage dispute – *chin-age tōsō* (cheen-ah-gay toe-so)

wage earner – *chingin shotoku sha* (cheen-gheen show-toe-kuu-shah)

wage freeze – *chingin tōketsu* (cheen-gheen toe-kate-sue)

wage level – *chingin suijun* (cheen-gheen suu-ee-june)

wage-price spiral – *bukka to chingin no aku-junkan* (buke-kah to cheen-gheen no ah-kuu-june-kahn)

wager – *kakegoto* (kah-kay-go-toe); *kake* (kah-kay)

wage regulations – *chingin kisoku* (cheen-gheen kee-so-kuu)

wage scale – *chingin sukēru* (cheen-gheen sue-kay-rue)

wage structure – *kyūyo kōzō* (cue-yoe koe-zoe)

waiver clause – *menseki jōkō* (men-say-kee joe-koe)

waiver clause for insurance – *kiken yakkan* (kee-ken yahk-kahn)

wake-up telephone call – *mezamashi denwa* (may-zah-mah-she den-wah)

I would like a 6 o'clock wake-up call.
  Roku-ji ni mezamashi denwa wo onegai shimasu.
  (roe-kuu-jee nee may-zah-mah-she den-wah oh oh-nay-guy she-mahss)

walkout (strike) – *sutoraiki* (stow-rye-kee)

want ad – *shinbun boshū kōkoku* (sheem-boon boe-shuu koe-koe-kuu)

warehouse – *sōko* (so-koe)

warehouseman – *sōko gyōsha* (so-koe g'yoe-shah)

warn – *chūi suru* (chew-ee sue-rue)

warrant (legal document) – *rei jō* (ray joe)

warrant (security) – *hoshō jō* (hoe-show joe)

warranty – *hoshō* (hoe-show)

warranty period – *hoshō kikan* (hoe-show kee-kahn)

wasted asset – *genmō shisan* (gen-moe she-sahn)

waybill – *kamotsu unsō jō* (kah-moat-sue uun-so joe)

weak point – *nigate na* (nee-gah-tay nah)

wealth – *zaisan* (zye-sahn)

wear and tear – *shōmō mason* (show-moe mah-soan)

weekly pay – *shū kyū* (shuu cue)

weekly returns – *shū eki* (shuu ay-kee)

weight – *jūryō* (juu-rio); *mekata* (may-kah-tah); gross weight – *sōjūryō* (so-juu-rio); net weight – *shōmiryō* (show-me-rio)

weighted average – *kajū heikin* (kah-juu hay-keen)

welcome (as on sign) – *go-kangei shimasu* (go-kahn-gay she-mahss); welcome speech – *kangei no enzetsu* (kahn-gay no en-zate-sue)

Western food – *yōshoku* (yoe-show-kuu)
  Let's eat Western food today.
  Kyō wa yōshoku wo tabemashō.
  (k'yoe wah yoe-show-kuu oh tah-bay-mah-show)

wheel (vehicle) – *sharin* (shah-reen)

white collar worker – *howaito karā* (hoe-why-toe kah-rah)

White Paper (issued by the government) – *Haku Sho* (hah-kuu show)

whole country – *zenkoku* (zen-koe-kuu)

wholesale – *oroshi-uri* (oh-roe-she-uu-ree)

wholesale market – *oroshi-uri shijō* (oh-roe-she-uu-ree she-joe)

wholesale price – *oroshi-uri kakaku* (oh-roe-she-uu-ree kah-kah-kuu)

wholesaler – *oroshi-uri gyōsha* (oh-roe-she-uu-ree g'yoe-shah); *oroshiya* (oh-roe-she-yah); *ton'ya* (tone-yah); primary wholesaler – *dai-ichi ton'ya* (dye-ee-chee tone-yah)

wholesale trade – *oroshi-uri gyō* (oh-roe-she-uu-ree g'yoe)

windfall profits – *gūhatsu rieki* (guu-hot-sue ree-ay-kee)

window dressing – *funshoku suru* (fuun-show-kuu sue-rue)

windshield – *furonto garasu* (fuu-roan-toe gah-rah-sue)

wire (metal) – *harigane* (hah-ree-gah-nay)

wire transfer – *denshin gawase* (den-sheen gah-wah-say)

withdraw (take out, pull out) – *hikidasu* (hee-kee-dah-sue)

withhold (at source) – *gensen chōshū* (gen-sen choe-shuu)

withholding tax – *gensen kazei* (gen-sen kah-zay)

witness – *shōnin* (show-neen)

word-processor – *wāpuro* (wah-puu-roe)

work (to work) – *hataraku* (hah-tah-rah-kuu)

work (job) – *shigoto* (she-go-toe)

workaholic – *shōbai nesshin na* (show-by nay-sheen nah); *shigoto chūdoku no* (she-go-toe chuu-doe-kuu no)

work committee – *kōjō iinkai* (koe-joe ee-een-kye)

work conditions – *rōdō jōken* (roe-doe joe-ken)

work council – *rōshi kyōgi kai* (roe-she k'yoe-ghee kye)

work cycle – *shigoto saikuru* (she-go-toe sigh-kuu-rue)

workday – *shūgyō-bi* (shuu-g'yoe-bee)

work force – *rōdō ryoku* (roe-doe rio-kuu)

work (operation) – *sagyō suru* (sah-g'yoe sue-rue)

working capital – *unten shihon* (uun-ten she-hone)

working class – *rōdō sha kaikyū* (roe-doe shah kye-cue)

working contract – *kōji keiyaku* (koe-jee kay-yah-kuu)

working funds – *unten shikin* (uun-ten she-keen)

working hours – *rōdō jikan* (roe-doe jee-kahn)

working papers – *kansa chōsho* (kahn-sah choe-show)

work in progress – *shikakari hin* (she-kah-kah-ree heen)

workload – *shigoto ryō* (she-go-toe rio)

work on contract – *keiyaku ni yoru shigoto* (kay-yah-kuu nee yoe-rue she-go-toe)

work order – *mitsumori shirei sho* (meet-sue-moe-ree she-ray-show)

workplace – *shigoto-ba* (she-go-toe-bah)

workshop – *sagyō-jō* (sah-g'yoe-joe)

workstation – *wāku sutēshon* (wah-kuu stay-shone)

World Bank – *Sekai Ginkō* (say-kye gheen-koe)

worthless – *kachi no nai* (kah-chee no nigh)

worth, net – *shōmi shisan* (show-me she-sahn)

writ – *rei jō* (ray joe)

write-down – *hyōka-gen* (h'yoe-kah-gen)

write off – *chōkeshi ni suru* (choe-kay-she nee sue-rue)

written agreement – *keiyaku sho* (kay-yah-kuu show)

written bid – *kin'yū nyūsatsu* (keen-yuu n'yuu-saht-t'sue)

— X —

x-ray examination – *ekkusu kōsen kensa* (ek-kuu-suu koe-sen ken-sah); *rentogen kensa* (ren-toe-gen ken-sah)

I had an x-ray taken this year.

Kotoshi rentogen kensa ukemashita.

(koe-toe-she ren-toe-gen ken-sah uu-kay-mahsh-tah)

x-rays – *ekkusu kōsen* (ek-kuu-suu koe-sen)

— Y —

yacht – *yotto* (yote-toe)
yard (measure) – *yādo* (yah-doe)
yardstick (figurative usage) – *handan no kijun* (hahn-dahn no kee-june)
year – *toshi* (toe-she)
year, fiscal – *kaikei nendo* (kye-kay nen-doe)
year-end – *nenmatsu no* (nen-mah-t'sue no)
yen – *en* (en)
yen terms – *en de* (en day)
yield – *rimawari* (ree-mah-wah-ree)
yield-to-maturity – *manki rimawari* (mahn-kee ree-mah-wah-ree)

— Z —

zero – *zero* (zay-roe)
zero-coupon – *zero kūpon sai* (zay-roe kuu-poan sigh)
ZIP Code – *yūbin bangō* (yuu-bean bahn-go)
zone (region) – *chiiki* (chee-ee-kee)
zoom lens – *zūmu renzu* (zuu-muu ren-zuu)